Acting Edition

PRISONER OF THE CROWN

THE ROYAL RAPE OF RUARI MACASMUNDE

BY RICHARD F. STOCKTON

ADDITIONAL MATERIAL AND ORIGINAL CONCEPT
BY RICHARD T. HERD

DPS

DRAMATISTS PLAY SERVICE

ISBN 978-0-8222-2352-8

www.dramatists.com

www.concordtheatricals.com

Note on Songs/Recordings, Images, or Other Production Design Elements

Be advised that Concord Theatricals neither holds the rights to nor grants permission to use any songs, recordings, images, or other design elements mentioned in the play. It is the sole responsibility of the producing theater/organization to obtain permission of the copyright owner(s) for any such use. Additional royalty fees may apply for the right to use copyrighted materials.

For any songs/recordings, images, or other design elements mentioned in the play, works in the public domain may be substituted. It is the producing theater/organization's sole responsibility to ensure the substituted work is indeed in the public domain. Concord Theatricals cannot advise as to whether or not a song/arrangement/recording, image, or other design element is in the public domain.

AUTHOR'S NOTE

This play concerns the life, trial for life and death of the last knight of the British realm hanged for high treason.

It takes place in the jury room at the Old Bailey and elsewhere in the minds of twelve jurors who reenact key events during their deliberation.

PRISONER OF THE CROWN was originally presented by The Abbey Theatre, in Dublin, Ireland, opening on February 15, 1972. It was directed by Tomas Mac Anna; the set design was by Brian Collins; the lighting design was by Leslie Scott; the costume design was by Josie Lovell; and the stage manager was Tommy Woods. The cast was as follows:

FIRST JUROR/SIR FREDERICK SMITH .... Bill Foley

SECOND JUROR/THE MILITARY POLICE SERGEANT/FIRST TOWER GUARD/MR. ALLEN/ PARCHMENT ATTENDANT/VICE PRESIDENT OF THE UNITED STATES/FATHER CAREY .... Bob Carlile

THIRD JUROR/FATHER RYAN/SENATOR WILLIAMS/HOME SECRETARY .... Michael Duffy

FOURTH JUROR/COMMISSIONER BASIL THOMPSON/SERGEANT SULLIVAN/ SIR ARTHUR CONAN DOYLE .... Geoffrey Golden

FIFTH JUROR/SERGEANT HEARN/ SIR EMLEY BLACKWELL .... Patrick McLoughlin

SIXTH JUROR/CONSTABLE RILEY/ SECOND TOWER GUARD/PRIVATE EGAN/ WAITER/ROLLS CLERK .... Paddy O'Callaghan

SEVENTH JUROR/LORD READING/ KEEPER OF THE ROLLS .... Harry Brogan

EIGHTH JUROR/ SIR ROGER CASEMENT .... John Kavanagh

NINTH JUROR/WELSH SENTRY/ PRIVATE NEILL AMERICAN REPORTER/ SECOND PARCHMENT ATTENDANT/ ARTEMUS JONES/JUNIOR COUNSEL .... Desmond Cave

TENTH JUROR/PRIVATE ROBINSON/SENATOR FROM OREGON/PROFESSOR MORGAN/ DOCTOR PRENTISS .... Joe Dowling

ELEVENTH JUROR/INSPECTOR QUINN/ MR. SHORTER/SIR EDWARD GREY .... Philip O'Flynn

TWELFTH JUROR/CAPTAIN HALL/ PRISON GOVERNOR .... Edward Golden

PRISONER OF THE CROWN received its North American premiere as *The Royal Rape of Ruari Macasmunde*, by the Virginia Museum Theatre, in Richmond, Virginia, opening on March 2, 1973. It was directed by Alfred Drake; the set design was by deTeel Patterson Tiller; the costume design was by André Bruce Ward; and the lighting design was by Michael Watson. The cast was as follows:

FIRST JUROR/INSPECTOR QUINN/
SIR FREDERICK SMITH .... Michael Miller

SECOND JUROR/SERGEANT HEARN/MILITARY POLICE
SERGEANT/SIR EMLEY BLACKWELL .... Colin Hamilton

THIRD JUROR/CAPTAIN HALL/SMITH'S/
ASSISTANT/ATTORNEY/SENATOR
WILLIAMS/EXECUTIONER .... Ken Letner

FOURTH JUROR/LORD READING/
COMMISSIONER/BASIL THOMPSON/
WELSH SENTRY/KEEPER OF THE ROLLS ...... Norman Barrs

FIFTH JUROR/MR. ALLEN/PROFESSOR MORGAN/
SENATOR STONE/PRISON GOVERNOR ..... W.R. Hutchinson

SIXTH JUROR/FATHER RYAN/COURTROOM
GUARD/MR. SHORTER/VICE PRESIDENT OF
THE UNITED STATES/HOME SECRETARY .... Ron Burn

SEVENTH JUROR/CONSTABLE RILEY/PRIVATE
EGAN/SHORTHAND CLERK/SECOND PARCHMENT
ATTENDANT/SENATE PAGE .... James Kirkland

EIGHTH JUROR/SECOND TOWER GUARD/
COURT CLERK/PRIVATE NEILL .... Mel Cobb

NINTH JUROR/FIRST TOWER GUARD/
PRIVATE ROBINSON/FIRST PARCHMENT ATTENDANT/
DR. PRENTISS/ROLLS CLERK .... Sam Maupin

TENTH JUROR/SHORTHAND CLERK/
ARTEMUS JONES/MR. SWEET/
JOHN/SENATOR FROM OREGON .... J. Michael Costello

ELEVENTH JUROR/MR. SULLIVAN/
SIR ARTHUR CONAN DOYLE/LORD GREY .... Gene Snow

TWELFTH JUROR/SIR ROGER CASEMENT .... Keith Fowler

PRISONER OF THE CROWN was subsequently produced by the Milwaukee Repertory Theater, in Milwaukee, Wisconsin, opening on October 5, 1973. It was directed by Nagle Jackson; the set and lighting designs were by Christopher M. Idoine; the costume design was by James Edmund Brady; and the production stage manager was Merry Tigar. The cast was as follows:

JUROR/CASEMENT .... Robert Lanchester

JUROR/MILITARY POLICE SERGEANT/
PRISONER NEILL/DR. PRENTISS WARDER .... Jim Baker

JUROR/HALL/DOCTOR .... Montgomery Davis

JUROR/RYAN/SHORTER/COURT CLERK ..... Robert Dawson

JUROR/KEEPER OF ROLLS/
SCOTLAND YARD CLERK/FIRST TOWER
GUARD/FIRST PARCHMENT GUARD/
AMERICAN REPORTER .... Robert Ground

JUROR/SMITH .... Robert Jorge

JUROR/SULLIVAN/CONSTABLE RILEY/
PRISON GOVERNOR .... Durward McDonald

JUROR/BLACKWELL .... William McKereghan

JUROR/READING/THOMSON/
HERBERT SAMUEL .... David O. Petersen

JUROR/SENTRY/SERGEANT HEARN/
TOWER SENTRY/PRISONER EGAN/
MORGAN/RECORDS CLERK .... Michael Pierce

JUROR/QUINN/ALLEN/EDWARD GREY/
SECOND PARCHMENT GUARD .... Richard Risso

JUROR/ROBINSON/ARTEMIS JONES/
SECOND TOWER GUARD .... Jack Swanson

BAILIFF .... Nagle Jackson

CUSTODIAN .... Ray Johnston

A reading of PRISONER OF THE CROWN was given at The Players Club in New York City on January 23 2008. It was directed by Robert Kalfin, and the assistant director was Mitchell Sawyer. The cast was as follows:

CHORUS .... Marcel Simoneau
READING/READING JUROR .... Burt Edwards
BAILIFF/GOVERNOR .... Peter Cormican
SIR FREDERICK SMITH/SMITH JUROR ..... SamTsoutsouvas
SIR ROGER CASEMENT/
CASEMENT JUROR .... Paul Schoeffler
SARGEANT SULLIVAN/SULLIVAN JUROR ..... Jack Davidson
M.P. JUROR/DOCTOR .... Sam Guncler
SIR ERNLEY BLACKWELL/BLACKWELL JUROR/
KEEPER OF THE ROLLS .... Kenneth Garner
SERGEANT HEARN/FIRST GUARD (ACT I)/
REPORTER SWEET/SHORTHAND CLERK .... Ben Rauch
INSPECTOR QUINN/QUINN JUROR/NEILL/
REPORTER SHORTER/FIRST GUARD (ACT II)/
SIR EDWARD GREY .... Chris Mixon
CAPTAIN REGINALD HALL/HALL JUROR ... Tony Newfield
FATHER RYAN/RYAN JUROR/JONES .... Frank Anderson
M.P. SERGEANT/RICHARD MORTON .... John Fitzgibbon
ROBINSON /ROBINSON JUROR/
SECOND GUARD .... Jonathan Phillips
CONSTABLE RILEY/SIR BASIL THOMPSON/
THOMPSON JUROR/REPORTER ALLEN/
MORGAN .... Michael Arkin
GERTRUDE .... Tamara Flanagan
STAGE DIRECTIONS .... Douglas Plaut

PRISONER OF THE CROWN received its New York premiere at the Irish Repertory Theater on May 22, 2008. It was directed by Ciaran O'Reilly; the set design was by Charlie Corcoran; the costume design was by David Toser; the lighting design was by Brian Nason; the sound design was by Zachary Williamson; the wig and hair designs were by Robert-Charles Vallance; the fight director was Rick Sordelet; the production stage manager was Elis Arroyo; and the stage manager was Leslie Grisdale. The cast was as follows:

BAILIFF/MILITARY POLICE OFFICER/RICHARD MORTON/MR. ALLEN/PROFESSOR MORGAN/ SIR EDWARD GREY/JUROR .... Peter Cormican

CHORUS/WELSH SENTRY/PARCHMENT GUARD/GERMAN GUARD/SECRETARY/ PRESS REPORTER/JUROR .... Patrick Fitzgerald

SIR RODGER CASEMENT/JUROR .... Philip Goodwin

GERTRUDE BANNISTER/FATHER RYAN/TOWER OF LONDON GUARD/ ARTEMUS JONES/JUROR .... Emma O'Donnell

BASIL THOMPSON/TOWER OF LONDON GUARD/SERGEANT SULLIVAN/JUROR .... Tim Ruddy

INSPECTOR QUINN/SIR ERNLEY BLACKWELL/ ROBINSON/MR. SHORTER/JUROR .... Ian Stuart

JUDGE READING/SERGEANT HEARN/ CAPTAIN REGINALD HALL/ EXECUTIONER/JUROR .... John C. Vennema

CONSTABLE RILEY/SIR FREDRICK SMITH/ NEILL (BLIND POW)/JUROR ...... John Windsor-Cunningham

CHARACTERS

BLACKWELL JUROR
CASEMENT JUROR
HALL JUROR
JUROR (BAKER)
M.P. JUROR
READING JUROR
ROBINSON JUROR
RYAN JUROR
SMITH JUROR
SULLIVAN JUROR
THOMPSON JUROR
ALLEN (PRESS)
AMERICAN REPORTER (PRESS)
BAILIFF
GERTRUDE BANNISTER
SIR ERNLEY BLACKWELL
BLACKWELL'S PAGE
SIR ROGER CASEMENT
CHORUS
CLERK (ROLLS OFFICE)
EXECUTIONER
FIRST PARCHMENT GUARD
FIRST TOWER GUARD
GERMAN POW GUARD
GOVERNOR (BRIXTON PRISON)
SIR EDWARD GREY
CAPTAIN REGINALD HALL
SERGEANT HEARN
ARTEMUS JONES
KEEPER OF THE ROLLS
M.P. SERGEANT

PROFESSOR MORGAN
RICHARD MORTON
NEILL (BLIND POW)
PRISON DOCTOR
PRISON WARDER
INSPECTOR QUINN
LORD READING
CONSTABLE RILEY
ROBINSON
FATHER RYAN
SECOND PARCHMENT GUARD
SECOND SHORTHAND CLERK
SENTRY (OLD BAILEY)
SHORTER (PRESS)
SHORTHAND CLERK
SIR FREDERICK SMITH
SMITH'S SECRETARY
SERGEANT SULLIVAN
BASIL THOMPSON
WELSH SENTRY (TAFFEY)

PLACE

A jury room at the Old Bailey and in the minds of the jurors.

TIME

The afternoon of June 9th, 1916.

CASTING NOTE

The Chorus, a stage character borrowed from Elizabethan drama, serves as an all-purpose narrator, musical director and stage manager, while also performing various bit parts.

There are numerous speaking roles as well as groups referred to as Jurors, Prisoners, Press Officials, etc. All can be performed by a dozen or so highly versatile actors who play other roles in addition to their identities as Jurors.

Certain dual roles are indicated for thematic consistency. Although the assignment of remaining roles can be adjusted to the resourcefulness, range, agility and dialect skills of actors, the following is one feasible distribution:

CHORUS
JUROR (BAKER)
SHORTHAND CLERK
WELSH SENTRY (TAFFEY)
SENTRY (OLD BAILEY)
SECOND PARCHMENT GUARD
SMITH'S SECRETARY
BLACKWELL'S PAGE
PRISON WARDER
CLERK (ROLLS OFFICE)

SIR ROGER CASEMENT
CASEMENT JUROR

SIR FREDERICK SMITH
SMITH JUROR
NEILL (BLIND POW)

SIR ERNLEY BLACKWELL
BLACKWELL JUROR
GERMAN POW GUARD

LORD READING
READING JUROR
SERGEANT HEARN

SHORTER (PRESS)
GOVERNOR (BRIXTON PRISON)

CAPTAIN REGINALD HALL
HALL JUROR
EXECUTIONER

GERTRUDE BANNISTER

BASIL THOMPSON
THOMPSON JUROR
PROFESSOR MORGAN
KEEPER OF THE ROLLS

SERGEANT SULLIVAN
SULLIVAN JUROR
CONSTABLE RILEY
SIR EDWARD GREY
PRISON DOCTOR

M.P. SERGEANT
M.P JUROR
FIRST TOWER GUARD
FIRST PARCHMENT GUARD

RICHARD MORTON
BAILIFF
INSPECTOR QUINN

FATHER RYAN
RYAN JUROR
ARTEMUS JONES
ALLEN (PRESS)

ROBINSON
ROBINSON JUROR
SECOND SHORTHAND CLERK
AMERICAN REPORTER (PRESS)

PRISONER OF THE CROWN

ACT ONE

We see a dimly lit multilevel stage with a few basic forms that will serve as tables, benches, cots, etc.

As house lights fade, we hear from offstage the strumming of a plaintive ballad on a guitar.

The Chorus, a pleasant young man, strolls onstage strumming and looking over the set. When he notices the audience, he stops playing, shrugs with a good-natured grin, then gestures with his guitar all around the set.

CHORUS. Doesn't tell you much, does it? I mean about where you are. And what it all means. *(Sly wink.)* So, it's a good thing *I'm* here, don't you think? This is all about an Irish patriot — or an English traitor — take your pick — who was hanged by the British in 1916. Nothing unusual there. Right? Plenty of dead Irish to choose from. Nothing special about this one. Right? *(Shakes his head.) Wrong!* Because *this* Irishman was "Sir" Roger David Casement. That's right — *Sir* Roger. The very last *knight* of the British realm ever to be hanged for high treason. *(Strums a somber guitar chord.)* But was he *really* hanged for treason? *(He glances into the wings to be sure no one is watching, then steps to the apron to confide his suspicion to the audience.)* Or was it for something else entirely? That's the question to be decided here. *(He strums another chord, then turns upstage to indicate the jury room area, as lights there fade up, then down.)* As you'll see in a jury room of the Old Bailey — just there — twelve jurors — true

Englishmen all — will deliberate scarce an hour before finding him guilty of treason. But is that truly the reason they hanged Sir Roger? *(Strums another chord.)* That's something *you* will have to decide for yourself. Of course, I have my own views on the matter … *(Sings.)*

O lordly Roger Casement,
you gave all a man could give
That justice be not mocked at
and that liberty might live.
But you hurt the high and mighty ones
in pocket and in pride
And that is why they hated you,
and that is why you died.

But I'll keep my own views to myself. *(Conspiratorial wink.)* That's the only fair way. Right? *(Points.)* Oh, that up there's the high bench. His Lordship is about to charge the jury. *(He turns to watch Lord Reading donning his peruke and adjusting his robe. Sings.)*

Aye, they stripped you of your honors
and they hounded you to death
And their blood lust was not sated
as you gasped your dying breath.
They tried to foul your memory
as they burned your corpse with lime.
But God is not an Englishman
and truth will out in time.

READING. Gentlemen, you have now heard all the evidence in the case of our Sovereign Lord and King against Sir Roger David Casement. The prisoner is accused of the gravest crime known to law — high treason. It is now for you to decide if he went into German prisoner-of-war camps and urged the Irish prisoners held there to return with him and raise a civil insurrection against the Crown in their Irish homeland. I instruct you, as a matter of British law, that neither the wisdom of his judgment nor the failure of his enterprise is at issue. The act, itself, is sufficient to convict. Are there questions? *(No response.)* Gentlemen, the prisoner stands at the bar for his deliverance. You may retire to the jury room to consider your verdict. *(Lights cross-fade from the high bench to the jury room. As the weary Jurors file in, several loosen their ties and remove their jackets. A disgruntled Bailiff counts heads.)*

BAILIFF. … Eight … nine … ten … eleven … *twelve* good men and true, as the statute says. Make yourselves at home, gentlemen.

There's water in the pitcher. A potty behind that door. If you want anything else, rap me in. When you've reached a verdict, don't be shy with it. Sing out! *(The Bailiff leaves, then immediately sticks his head back in for a parting shot.)* He's *guilty!* No mistake about that. You could see it in his eyes. So let's have no mucking about, gentlemen. No mucking about. *(The Bailiff leaves. The Jurors glance around at each other self-consciously.)*
SMITH JUROR. Well … as foreman, I suggest we take a vote straightaway.
CASEMENT JUROR. Why?
SMITH JUROR. To see where we stand and what we're up against.
CASEMENT JUROR. With no discussion?
SMITH JUROR. We'll come to discussion, if there's a need for it.
CHORUS. I feel some need for it now.
SMITH JUROR. Are there anymore of you?
SULLIVAN JUROR. I have a few questions on points that weren't altogether clear. To *me,* anyway.
SMITH JUROR. *(Annoyed.)* That's three, then. *(Knows it'll be a long session, Smith Juror sheds his jacket and opens his collar.)*
M.P. JUROR. Look 'ere! We all heard the same evidence and it's perfectly clear to us. Why ain't it clear to *'im?*
BLACKWELL JUROR. Not everyone has your obvious facility for crisp, analytical thinking.
M.P. JUROR. 'Ere now. Was that a put-down, Gov?
BLACKWELL JUROR. Not at all. I agree with you entirely. Of course, he's guilty.
SULLIVAN JUROR. But guilty of *what?*
M.P. JUROR. Betrayin' 'is country.
SULLIVAN JUROR. Ireland, you mean?
M.P. JUROR. *England!*
SULLIVAN JUROR. *(Innocently.)* Oh? Was he born in England?
M.P. JUROR. No. Ulster. But he still —
SULLIVAN JUROR. His parents, then?
M.P. JUROR. Not as I know. But that doesn't mean —
SULLIVAN JUROR. His relatives, perhaps? From Yorkshire were they? Cheshire?
M.P. JUROR. No!
SULLIVAN JUROR. Did he invade England? Sail up the Thames with a small armada?
M.P. JUROR. Of course not! All the same, he had no business —

SULLIVAN JUROR. Wait! I have it! He put an Irish garrison in the streets of London to scatter children on their way to school. To nip a morning shopper now and then with a stray bullet.
M.P. JUROR. That's not the point! And you bloody well know it!
SULLIVAN JUROR. *(Coolly.)* Not really. That's the part I'm unclear about. Good to know you've got it all sorted out, though.
SMITH JUROR. I still think a pro forma vote is the way to start. Just a formality. You don't have to identify yourself. *(Smith Juror passes out blank ballots. Hall Juror collects the marked and folded ballots and hands them to Reading Juror, who makes two piles.)*
M.P. JUROR. *(Still rankled.)* You don't fancy the likes of me 'avin' a vote just as good as yours, do you?
SULLIVAN JUROR. Not really … no. *(M.P. Juror defiantly slaps down his ballot in front of Reading Juror.)*
READING JUROR. "Guilty"! … That makes nine for conviction. Two for acquittal. And one blank. *(Smith Juror grabs it and looks on both sides, disgusted.)*
SMITH JUROR. There's always one that's neither fish nor fowl. Whose is it?
CASEMENT JUROR. Mine.
SMITH JUROR. Come on, be a good chap. Guilty? Or not guilty?
CASEMENT JUROR. I don't know yet …
SMITH JUROR. We're not asking you to have *our* opinion. But you must have one of your *own!*
CASEMENT JUROR. I don't … not yet …
M.P. JUROR. When *do* you have opinions, then? Every other Tuesday? On Guy Fawkes Day?
SMITH JUROR. We have to start with *something,* man!
CASEMENT JUROR. Couldn't we go over it again? Carefully? In detail?
HALL JUROR. We've *been* over it! Out there in court. For three days.
CASEMENT JUROR. There may be something they overlooked.
M.P. JUROR. Them? Sir Freddy Smith, Lord Reading and all those toffs? Not bloody likely.
ROBINSON JUROR. Must we go over it all again? Just for you?
CASEMENT JUROR. It's a man's *life* …
CHORUS. And Sir Roger could be right, you know!
SMITH JUROR. About *what?*

CHORUS. That he should have been tried in Ireland. Not here — by *foreigners!*

M.P. JUROR. What's that? Us? Foreigners?

HALL JUROR. We're all Englishmen same as himself.

CASEMENT JUROR. That's just the point. He's not English. He's Irish.

READING JUROR. No difference. Same king. One Empire.

CASEMENT JUROR. If you believe that, then you must treat him fairly, as a fellow Englishman.

ROBINSON JUROR. A traitor like 'im? Not bloody likely.

RYAN JUROR. Be a good chap, now. Put down your vote.

CASEMENT JUROR. No. I … I can't … *(Casement Juror rips, drops his ballot.)*

ROBINSON JUROR. Awwww. You didn't have to tear it up.

M.P. JUROR. Feels superior, 'e does. Not like the rest of us.

CASEMENT JUROR. That's not so. It's just that —

M.P. JUROR. Just what? Go on!

CASEMENT JUROR. It's just that … you're making a mistake … *(Note: first transition. Casement Juror retreats from the taunting Jurors to an area representing the shore of Tralee Bay. The sound of surf sneaks in. Constable Riley is behind him, piecing together the torn ballot.)*

CASEMENT. … A terrible mistake, Constable.

RILEY. *(Pleasant, but wary.)* That's as may be, Sir. But you deliberately tore up this paper when you saw me coming. It could be evidence.

CASEMENT. Of what? What am I supposed to have done?

RILEY. That's not for me to say, Sir. *(Reads.)* "Left Wicklow in Willie's yacht. Willie's yacht broke down." It appears to be some kind of code.

CASEMENT. *(Amused.)* It's a poem, Constable.

RILEY. A poem? This?

CASEMENT. Allegorical, I'm afraid. The days of "Many and many a year ago, In a kingdom by the sea" are quite gone, Constable — uh — ?

RILEY. Riley, sir.

CASEMENT. Are you acquainted with modern verse, Constable Riley?

RILEY. No. And I'm not acquainted with *you,* either. Who are you?

CASEMENT. Just a typical English traveler on a morning stroll down the beach. Anything wrong with that?

RILEY. Your shoes is wet.
CASEMENT. I strolled too near the surf.
RILEY. Your trousers, too. Soakin' wet. And your coat.
CASEMENT. I was taken unawares by your famous tide of Tralee, Constable Riley. You know how we poets are — heads in the clouds. I'm lucky I wasn't drowned.
HEARN. Perhaps! *(Casement whirls to find another police officer behind him.)*
CASEMENT. You have very soft feet, Sergeant.
RILEY. 'E says 'e's an allegorical poet takin' the mornin' air.
CASEMENT. Yes. I find your Irish sea breeze invigorating. Perhaps more Dionysian than Apollonian, but nonetheless —
HEARN. What are you *really* doing here?
CASEMENT. By what authority do you ask?
HEARN. I can arrest you under the Defence of the Realm Act.
CASEMENT. Are poets now considered a threat to the realm, Sergeant?
HEARN. In time of war, anyone who goes swimming before breakfast can be a threat. What's your name?
CASEMENT. Richard Morton. *(At a nod from Hearn, Riley takes out a notepad to record answers.)*
HEARN. Where do you live?
CASEMENT. The Savoy. Denham, Buckinghamshire.
HEARN. Occupation?
CASEMENT. *(Wryly.)* Why is it always assumed that an author must have another occupation?
HEARN. Name me a book you've written.
CASEMENT. *The Life of St. Brenden.*
HEARN. *(Challenging.)* It so happens I've read that book.
CASEMENT. I wish there were more of you. My royalties were meager.
HEARN. It's a fine book.
CASEMENT. Thank you, Sergeant. I must remember to send you my gratitude on a fly-leaf.
RILEY. 'E's writin' modern verses, now. 'Ere's one 'e tore up. *(Hearn fits two pieces together, then frowns suspiciously.)*
HEARN. Who's "Willie"?
CASEMENT. William the Conqueror.
HEARN. On a *yacht?*
CASEMENT. A symbol for the Ship of State.

HEARN. Hm … It's not a very good poem.
CASEMENT. That's why I tore it up.
HEARN. Well, maybe Inspector Quinn at Police Barracks will appreciate it more. He's a Trinity man. Let's try it on him, shall we? *(Hearn motions Casement to walk ahead of him. Surf sounds fade out. They cross into an area where Inspector Quinn is waiting. Hearn takes off Casement's jacket and searches the pockets.)*
QUINN. At which port did you reach Ireland, Mr. Morton?
CASEMENT. Have you sent for a priest yet?
QUINN. When did you land?
CASEMENT. I believe it is my right to speak with a priest.
QUINN. For a "poet," you seem well versed on the niceties of law.
CASEMENT. Not all poets are wild visionaries, Inspector.
QUINN. *(Heavy irony.)* No. And in Ireland, not all wild visionaries are poets. I've sent for the barracks chaplain, Father Ryan.
CASEMENT. Thank you. I reached Dublin at eight o'clock this morning.
QUINN. Have you a passport, then?
CASEMENT. Why would I need a passport to travel within the Empire?
QUINN. *Any* papers for identification?
CASEMENT. Nothing on me, I'm afraid. *(Hearn finds something in Casement's jacket pocket and passes it to Quinn.)*
QUINN. Mr. Morton, when were you last in Germany?
CASEMENT. 1908, I believe … researching a new book.
QUINN. I meant *recently.*
CASEMENT. I take no great interest in politics. But unless I'm badly misinformed, we've been at *war* with Germany for two years.
QUINN. *Some* of us … yes.
CASEMENT. If that was a legal charge, you'll have to be more specific.
QUINN. You are a German spy, put ashore at Tralee during the night from … *(Checks the torn paper.)* from Kaiser "Willie's" yacht.
CASEMENT. Well, that is *specific.* But sheer fantasy.
QUINN. How did you get here from Dublin this morning?
CASEMENT. The early train.
QUINN. Ah, then you must have a railway stub…?
CASEMENT. Conductors take them up, I believe.
QUINN. Not always. This one was still in your jacket pocket.

"Prussich-Hessiche Staats Eisenbahnen." The Prussian-Hessian National Railway. *"Bettkarte, Erste Classe."* First-class sleeping car. Dated last week. *"Von Berlin zu Wilhelmshaven."* Wilhelmshaven? The submarine base! So "Willie's yacht" was a submarine. *"Preis: zehn tausend fünfzig Mark."*

CASEMENT. A "costly" ticket.

QUINN. *Very* costly. *(Father Ryan enters.)*

RYAN. You sent for me, Inspector?

QUINN. Yes. Mr. "Morton" here will be charged under the Defence of the Realm Act. Will you talk with him?

RYAN. Of course. *(Quinn and Hearn withdraw.)*

CASEMENT. Father Ryan, you're a priest and you're Irish. I have no choice but to put my absolute trust in you.

RYAN. That's why I'm here, Mr. Morton.

CASEMENT. I am Roger Casement.

RYAN. Yes?

CASEMENT. *Sir* Roger Casement! *(Father Ryan nods and offers his hand.)*

RYAN. Pleased to meet you. Patrick Ryan, Dominican.

CASEMENT. You really don't know me?

RYAN. Have we met?

CASEMENT. No. But I thought — No matter. The point is a German U-boat brought me here. So they think I'm a spy.

RYAN. Are you?

CASEMENT. No, Father. Of course not.

RYAN. Then why were you in Germany?

CASEMENT. To secure a treaty that will guarantee Irish independence after the war.

RYAN. You can't trust the Germans to honor such a treaty.

CASEMENT. Then whose honor *can* we trust? The English?

RYAN. Sooner than the Germans.

CASEMENT. Then God save Ireland!

RYAN. Amen.

CASEMENT. Father, you must get a message to the rebels in Dublin to call off the uprising set for Easter morning.

RYAN. I can't do that, Sir Roger. I'm trusted here.

CASEMENT. You don't understand. Pearse and MacNeill are counting on me to return with a brigade of Irish soldiers from German prison camps. But there *is* no brigade. You must warn them.

RYAN. Impossible. I've given the British my oath — as a priest.

CASEMENT. Would you give them the best blood in Ireland to go with it? There's no one else to head them off.
RYAN. But I am a man of God!
CASEMENT. Then in God's name — warn them, Father! I'm not asking you to *start* a mass killing — but to *stop* one! Is there a more Christian business for any man of God? *(Pause.)* Father?
RYAN. *(Reluctant.)* Very well. I'll get your message to the right hands. *(Father Ryan backs out of the lighted area. Casement sinks, wearily, into Quinn's desk chair. Quinn appears behind him and gives the chair a hard push. It rolls on casters under a hot, white light, where it is caught and swung around and around by a gruff M.P. Sergeant.)*
SERGEANT. I don't think you're listening to me! *Are* you listening, then? *Are* you?
CASEMENT. I'm trying to … Sergeant. But I haven't slept for days … I'm afraid my mind is … What were you saying?
SERGEANT. I said give me your bootlaces!
CASEMENT. My … bootlaces?
SERGEANT. We wouldn't want you to hang *yourself,* would we? *(Casement unlaces and hands them over.)*
CASEMENT. With a bootlace?
SERGEANT. One is a lace. Two wound together is a rope. Now the tie. *(Casement surrenders his tie.)* And the braces. *(Impatient.)* Your *braces! (Casement stands up to unhook his suspenders in back, then starts to sit again, holding up his trousers.)*
SERGEANT. No, no! Stay up. And strip down. *(The Sergeant whips out a pair of rubber surgical gloves and stretches them on, popping the fingers one by one.)*
CASEMENT. Certainly *not.*
SERGEANT. It's for your own good. Prisoners have been known to hide poison pills — bits of saw blades —
CASEMENT. No!
SERGEANT. Did that sound like a question? You get a search skin-out before I take you to Scotland Yard. I don't care for it any more than you. Now strip!
CASEMENT. I refuse.
SERGEANT. Why?
CASEMENT. I do not choose to tell you. *(A slow smile comes over the Sergeant's face, as he pulls on the second glove.)*
SERGEANT. Well, Mr. Morton, we all do things we don't choose. I mean that's discipline, isn't it?

CASEMENT. I won't submit to it.
SERGEANT. Not willingly, perhaps. But you'll submit, all right. I *promise* you *that! (Other guards drift into the circle of light, surrounding Casement. He leaps out of the chair suddenly and tries to bolt between two of them. Guards fling him back into the chair. The ring tightens. The chair is spun around crazily, as the guards shield Casement from view. Casement's shirt comes flying out of the circle of struggling guards. Then his shoes. Casement jumps up, bare-chested, on the chair seat — trying to escape their grasping hands. He clings to his pants, as hands drag him down out of sight. The lights dim out along with Casement's long, despairing wail. In the dark, a projector casts a large blow-up photo of Casement on a wall. We are in Scotland Yard, with two officials, Basil Thompson, head of CID, and Captain Reginald Hall, of Naval Intelligence.)*
THOMPSON. That's him, beard and all.
HALL. There were no clean-shaven photographs in the Consular files. He wore a beard after his initial appointment in the Belgian Congo. Probably to affect more maturity. He was only thirty.
THOMPSON. Young for a full Consular post.
HALL. Yes. A brilliant Irish mind and a prominent Tory patron — always a potent combination. It was Sir Edward Grey who pushed him along. Here's Roger right after he was knighted. *(Another slide is projected.)*
THOMPSON. Thin. Emaciated, really.
HALL. Malaria. He was too weak to attend the ceremony.
THOMPSON. Why *was* he knighted?
HALL. For the devastating report he did on the brutalizing of Congolese natives. The ones on King Leopold's personal rubber plantations. He took these photographs as proof. *(Hall projects a series of atrocity photos. [1] A work-gang chained by their necks. [2] Natives displaying objects.)*
THOMPSON. What's that they're holding up?
HALL. Amputated hands. A standard punishment. *(Slide [3] Footless women on crutches. [4] A native locked in the stocks.)*
CHORUS. Holy Mother o' God … *(The Chorus reappears as a young Shorthand Clerk, unseen 'til now. He suddenly steps into the projector beam, casting his gesticulating shadow on the wall.)*
HALL. Yes, Corporal?
CHORUS. That's what Sir Roger done? Put an end to that kind of *butchery?*

HALL. Yes. And single-handed, too. Remarkable achievement. King Leopold couldn't show his face in public after. *(Slide [5] A native man contemplating a severed foot. Partly obscured by the mesmerized Chorus.)* Corporal? … *Corporal! (The Chorus comes to, and jumps back out of the projector beam.)*

CHORUS. Oh! Sorry, Sir!

THOMPSON. Is that a human *foot?*

HALL. Yes. All that remained of his five-year-old daughter.

THOMPSON. Where's the rest of her?

HALL. Eaten. The plantation guards were cannibals. Casement's report turned everyone's stomach at the time. *(Hall snaps off the projector. Area lights up.)*

THOMPSON. Was it seeing all those atrocities that affected his mind?

HALL. You think his mind was affected?

THOMPSON. Well, the man chucked a brilliant career in the Foreign Office to conspire with Germans.

HALL. Yes. But what makes you think his mind was affected?

THOMPSON. Dammit, man! He turned against the Empire, didn't he?

HALL. Thompson, how many years did you spend with burglars and pickpockets?

THOMPSON. Why? What did I say?

HALL. Sir Roger has the same brilliant mind he always had. Underestimate him and he'll outwit us both.

THOMPSON. He tried to get Irish war prisoners to fight against the Crown. If that's not treason enough to hang a man, what is?

HALL. *(Genuinely amazed.)* You actually think the important thing is to *hang* him?

THOMPSON. It isn't…? *(The M.P. Sergeant arrives, prodding a dazed and fatigued Casement ahead of him, still holding up his trousers.)*

SERGEANT. The Crown prisoner, sir.

HALL. Has he made any statement, Sergeant?

SERGEANT. No, sir. We came over on the mail boat. It was a very quiet crossing. I might even say … sullen.

HALL. I'll take charge of him, Sergeant. You're relieved.

SERGEANT. Thank you, sir. *(The M.P. Sergeant leaves. At a signal from Hall, the Chorus opens a pad and begins a verbatim transcript.)*

CASEMENT. *(Groggy.)* What day is it now?

HALL. Tuesday.

CASEMENT. Easter week?
THOMPSON. That's right.
HALL. Do you know where you are now?
CASEMENT. Scotland Yard. May I see today's newspaper?
HALL. I'm Captain Hall of Naval Intelligence. This is Commissioner Thompson of the Criminal Investigation Division. Your name?
CASEMENT. Am I allowed a visitor here?
HALL. It might be arranged. Who?
CASEMENT. Sir Edward Grey.
HALL. What makes you think the Foreign Secretary would visit you?
CASEMENT. He would come.
THOMPSON. You have very high placed friends for a poet, "Mr. Morton." Who are you *really?*
CASEMENT. Ruari MacAsmunde.
THOMPSON. That's a *lie!* You're Roger Casement! We've got photographs and handwriting to prove it!
HALL. *Thompson!*
THOMPSON. You may be willing to sit still for that kind of cheekiness, but I have no —
HALL. His name *is* Ruari MacAsmunde! That's proper Gaelic for "Roger Casement." Do you wish to volunteer a statement at this time, Sir Roger?
CASEMENT. I shall seek legal advice.
HALL. Do you recognize this sleeping car ticket from Berlin to Wilhelmshaven?
CASEMENT. It is not my property.
THOMPSON. It was found in the pocket of this jacket.
CASEMENT. The jacket is not my property.
THOMPSON. It matches the trousers you have on.
CASEMENT. The trousers are not mine.
THOMPSON. But you're *wearing* them!
CASEMENT. *(Sudden vehemence.)* I was *strip-searched! (Calmly.)* Someone exchanged them.
THOMPSON. *(Infuriated.)* Those are the same clothes you came ashore in! They're still *sandy,* for God's sake!
HALL. Sir Roger, this torn notepaper bears a coded message in your handwriting. An expert has already been to the Foreign Office to compare it with specimens from your Consular Reports.

CASEMENT. I wanted those read for *more* than my handwriting.
HALL. Indeed. Your compassion for the tyrannized blacks was most eloquent. Oppressed peoples seem to bring out your finest efforts.
CASEMENT. With too little effect, I'm afraid.
HALL. First the black Congolese.
CASEMENT. Yes.
HALL. Then the Peruvian natives.
CASEMENT. Yes.
HALL. Now the Irish. *(Casement is about to agree, when he notices the Chorus taking it down.)*
CASEMENT. I am prepared to answer for my own conduct. But I will discuss nothing that involves others in an "official" way.
HALL. *(To Chorus.)* That'll be all, Corporal. You may go. *(The Chorus closes his pad. On the way out he gives Casement a "thumbs up.")* A recent issue of the *New York World* says the Germans paid twelve thousand dollars in gold to betray England.
CASEMENT. You don't believe that for an instant.
THOMPSON. *I* believe it! I bloody well believe it!
CASEMENT. *(Icy disdain.)* Yes … you are just the sort who might. *(To Hall.)* I have never taken a single pfennig from the Germans. They offered it — but I refused. I left Germany poorer than I went in.
HALL. Then you *do* admit leaving Germany for Ireland?
CASEMENT. Between us? Certainly. May I see a newspaper now?
HALL. Are you anxious about something?
CASEMENT. Just curious. I've seen no papers since Good Friday.
HALL. Later, perhaps. *(Hall nods to Thompson to take over the interrogation. Hall circles around behind Casement and snaps his fingers. Another pool of light comes up revealing a Second Shorthand Clerk, who cannot be seen by Casement. He nods and starts writing.)*
THOMPSON. You came in a German submarine?
CASEMENT. The U-19. We started out in the U-20, but it had engine trouble.
THOMPSON. To lead an Irish insurrection? *(Casement merely smiles. Hall returns.)*
HALL. If the Germans really meant well, wouldn't they have sent along some Krauts to help you?
CASEMENT. Germany is fighting a desperate battle for her own life.
HALL. Have you considered the possibility that what the Germans

really want is a military diversion in England's backyard — and don't give a *damn* about Irish independence?
CASEMENT. Possibly. To arrive at freedom, the route is unimportant.
THOMPSON. Doesn't it distress you that you have *failed?* That you have put your Irish neck in a British noose for nothing? *(Father Ryan enters, hesitantly. Casement is visibly cheered.)*
CASEMENT. You're mistaken. By calling off the general uprising set for Easter morning, I have saved hundreds of good Irish lives that will rise up to haunt you another day. My life for theirs? I struck a good bargain.
HALL. *(Deliciously.) Now* ... you may read a newspaper. *(Hall takes it out of his desk and drops it in front of Casement, who looks at it, horrified, then sags.)* I admire courage — but not stupidity. Cobblestones and pitchforks against machine guns. Connolly and Pearse were trapped in the post office and smoked out. They were both court martialed and shot by a firing squad.
THOMPSON. No Irish Brigade. No German help. And no hope. Your little adventure hasn't come to much, has it? *(Casement turns slowly to stare at Father Ryan with growing suspicion.)*
CASEMENT. So many died, Father.
RYAN. We must pray for them.
CASEMENT. I trusted you ... *(Suddenly, Casement flies at Father Ryan's throat. Hall and Thompson pull him away.)*
HALL. Don't blame Father Ryan.
CASEMENT. He told you everything!
HALL. Yes. But he took your order to Pearse *first.*
CASEMENT. *(To Father Ryan.)* You took it...? Then why wasn't it obeyed?
RYAN. Mr. Pearse said you have lived too long away from Ireland. That you have lived so well you have forgotten how to die well. But he would remind you. *(Casement is stunned. Hall dismisses Father Ryan with a gesture.)*
HALL. Tell us the names of the other rebel leaders, Sir Roger, so we can avert the next bloodbath before it begins. *(No response.)* The charge against you will be high treason.
CASEMENT. I trust so. *(Thompson whispers to Hall, who nods soberly, then turns to Casement.)*
HALL. Sir Roger, they've brought in some trunks you stored over in Ebery Street. But they're locked. Have you the keys?

CASEMENT. Break them open. There's nothing valuable. Old clothes — papers — the like. I've no further use of them. *(Thompson leaves.)*

HALL. Now, Sir Roger, I must ask you again for those names.

CASEMENT. I won't disgrace myself by naming anyone in the movement.

HALL. Need I remind you that you are a knight of the realm and a British subject?

CASEMENT. I have renounced both.

HALL. Perhaps I should explain the protection they afford you, as to the form of trial you will face.

CASEMENT. No matter. I would never claim "foreign" citizenship to protect myself. It's a matter of personal integrity. *(Offstage, there is a loud banging of trunks being broken into. Casement glances casually at the noise.)*

HALL. Yes … "personal integrity."

CASEMENT. You make it sound like a fault.

HALL. Not so much a fault as a … chink. Something to be pressed on. I assure you it's nothing personal, but it always puts my teeth on edge to meet a man of impeccable nobility. *(Thompson reenters, dusting off an old black ledger. He hands it to Hall, who shows an open page to Casement.)* Your handwriting, Sir Roger?

CASEMENT. Yes. My personal diary.

HALL. How "personal"?

CASEMENT. Judge for yourself.

HALL. You don't mind my browsing through it, then?

CASEMENT. Would that stop you?

HALL. Not really.

CASEMENT. Then go ahead, Captain … go right ahead and … *(Suddenly Casement loses his composure. He snatches the ledger from Hall's hands and retreats back into the Jury Room area, with Hall and Thompson pursuing.)*

CASEMENT JUROR. No! No! We can't use his diaries in our deliberations!

HALL JUROR. Why not?

CASEMENT JUROR. They were never introduced as evidence!

SULLIVAN JUROR. Exactly! So he had no opportunity to refute them.

CHORUS. He's right, you know. They were not in the trial.

HALL JUROR. Nonsense! They were *everywhere* in the trial.

Carefully planted in the back of everyone's mind.

SMITH JUROR. There's no way now to keep his diaries *out* of the trial.

QUINN JUROR. They hovered over the whole proceedings from first to last.

SULLIVAN JUROR. All the same, his private character is not the issue.

THOMPSON JUROR. That's bloody nonsense! I can't forget what he really is. Beneath all that Oxford polish and ramrod poise of his.

RYAN JUROR. I've got one like 'im in the shop. Won't give the packin' room boys a moment's peace. It gives me the shivers just to look at 'im, I can tell you.

READING JUROR. The only charge is "high treason." There's proof enough of that to hang him ten times over. We needn't to go into this other "detestable" business.

CASEMENT JUROR. Which, I remind you, was never offered in evidence — let alone *proved!*

M.P. JUROR. *Proved?* Did you take a good look at him in there — sitting cross-legged in the dock? All poised and proper. His hair spit down. His beard combed up. His eyes always slinkin' about the courtroom. I caught him starin' right into me once and I got the very same shivers —

BLACKWELL JUROR. I hardly think your thermal responses a suitable guide through the intricacies of statutory law.

M.P. JUROR. *(Hostile, suspicious.)* I don't know what that means.

BLACKWELL JUROR. Fair enough. I don't know what your shivering means, either. Can't we dispense with all this bickering and take another vote? *(Checks his pocket watch.)* I have a dinner engagement.

M.P. JUROR. I don't think your *appetite* is a suitable guide, either.

BLACKWELL JUROR. *(Thin smile.)* I stand reproved. Might we at least get off dead center and take a vote.

SMITH JUROR. Anyone object? *(No response.)* Right, then. Everyone take a paper and put down "guilty." *(Adds quickly.)* Or "*not* guilty." *(Hall Juror circles the area, collecting "secret" ballots and announcing results.)*

HALL JUROR. Guilty … guilty … very good … guilty … Oh, so you've changed your vote. It's "guilty" now, is it?

CHORUS. Of *treason! (To audience.)* Nothing else. *(To Hall.)* I've got a bakery to run that bloody well can't run itself. *(The Chorus wilts under Casement Juror's accusing look. Hall Juror takes Casement Juror's ballot and frowns at it.)*

HALL JUROR. Gentlemen … we *still* don't have a verdict.

ROBINSON JUROR. *(Utter disgust.)* Well, there it is.

M.P. JUROR. Every jury has got a blighter or two as loves to toss a spanner in the gears! *(M.P. Juror kicks over a chair and stalks away to fume. Other Jurors drift away in small groups, casting hostile glances at Casement Juror. Hall Juror hands the stack of ballots to Smith Juror, who flips through them, disappointed. Lights transpose to the House of Commons office of Attorney General Frederick E. Smith. Gertrude Bannister, Casement's devoted younger cousin, attractive and strong-willed, tries to remain composed.)*

GERTRUDE. I made the crossing as soon as I heard that Roger was in your custody. But they wouldn't tell me *where!* I've been shuttled from office to office —

SMITH. Who informed you he was in my custody, Miss Bannister?

GERTRUDE. That isn't the point —

SMITH. Father Ryan?

GERTRUDE. The point is you have him. We both know that. And I insist on seeing him at once!

SMITH. *Insist? At once?* You are not addressing one of your sullen school girls, Miss Bannister. I am Attorney General of England.

GERTRUDE. *(Backs down.)* I meant as soon as possible, Sir Frederick.

SMITH. Much better. Now fill out this visitor's request stating why you wish to see the prisoner.

GERTRUDE. I am his *cousin* — his *family!* Do I need more reason than that?

SMITH. Just fill it out, Miss Bannister. Your application will be processed along with the others.

GERTRUDE. Others? You mean to say no one's seen him? It's been four days! Surely he has seen an attorney?

SMITH. I don't believe he has one.

GERTRUDE. Then I will see that he does! And a good one! Roger has a great many friends who will not tolerate this treatment.

SMITH. Indeed? Put down their names, as well.

GERTRUDE. You won't need a list, Sir Frederick! You will hear from them directly! All of them!

SMITH. I await that with keen interest. Now, if you will excuse me, Miss Bannister, I do have "important" matters to attend to.

GERTRUDE. Sir Frederick, if I cannot see Roger today … would you kindly see that he gets this letter … so he will not think he has been totally abandoned.
SMITH. Of course.
GERTRUDE. Thank you. May I call tomorrow for my visitor's pass?
SMITH. It may take a bit longer. I'll send word to your hotel. *(Gertrude leaves the office and moves into a pool of light. Smith opens the sealed letter. As he reads it, Gertrude recites the contents.)*
GERTRUDE. "Dearest cousin … When I heard what happened I was appalled … and terribly concerned. I remember all the hours we spent as children dressed up in fancy costumes … fearless liberators freeing our homeland from heartless British tyrants … How we romped and swaggered until our glorious deeds were done … Then we put away our wooden swords and costumes … and the world went on its dreary way. When we grew up, I became a teacher and put away our dreams of glory. But you could not … and became a prisoner of the Crown.

"Dearest Roger … forgive me for leaving you to pursue our childhood dreams … alone. I promise never to desert you again. I have taken a leave of absence from St. Anne's to see you through this ordeal and safely back home in Ireland.

"I have already enlisted Mrs. Green to raise funds for your defence. Nearly one thousand pounds is already pledged. And a flood of letters from highly placed friends will descend on Downing Street. So be of good cheer until I bring you even better news … Your ever-adoring cousin, 'Gee.'" *(Lights fade on Gertrude. Smith smiles and locks the letter in his desk, as Hall enters and hands him pages to glance at.)*
SMITH. This is *all* you could get him to admit? Nothing more off the record?
HALL. That *is* off the record.
SMITH. Strange he didn't open up more. A man that self-righteous.
HALL. He admits coming over in the U-boat.
SMITH. Good enough to convict. Not good enough to *annihilate.* Despite centuries of evidence to the contrary, the Crown never meant to go into the business of manufacturing Irish martyrs.
HALL. At all events, we never supply enough to meet the demand.
SMITH. God knows. The right honorable gentlemen were frothing in Commons today. They'll demand my resignation, if I don't

arrange to have Sir Roger drawn and quartered in Hyde Park.

HALL. Yes. Nothing subverts an Englishman's legendary respect for fair play sooner than seeing it practiced.

SMITH. I met with the cabinet this evening. They were in a stew over a cable from Washington. The Senate is, by your leave, preparing a resolution to instruct us in our moral duty.

HALL. Incredible.

SMITH. Get the witnesses over from Ireland. I'll arrange for the "Irish Brigade" to be represented in the witness box. *(Afterthought.)* How's he holding up physically?

HALL. Remarkably well.

SMITH. *(Accusing.)* Why?

HALL. Sheer will-power, I expect.

SMITH. May I suggest The Tower?

HALL. *(Smiling.)* Of course …

SMITH. As a sensitive intellectual, he has certain fundamental needs. To communicate, for instance.

HALL. No newspapers. No stationery. No visitors.

SMITH. Personal cleanliness. An integrity of the body, as it were.

HALL. Cell four.

SMITH. Most critical to a man of Sir Roger's delicate mental constitution is the periodic need for *total* privacy. *(As Hall nods, lights cross-fade to the infamous Cell Four in the Tower of London. Casement, haggard and wretched in his rumpled, salt-stained clothes, is adrift between waking and sleeping on a filthy straw-pallet cot. Casement moans in this tortured state, trying to shield his eyes from the glare of a naked, overhead light bulb. Two unarmed Guards, seated on opposite sides of the cot, stare intently at him. The First Guard's head dips, then jerks up, as he fights to stay awake. The Second Guard goes methodically from finger to finger, cracking his knuckles. Nearby, with his back turned, the Chorus [now a young Welsh sentry with a rifle] is softly singing "My Little Welsh Home," a minor-key Welsh lullaby.)*

CHORUS.

I am dreaming of the mountains of my home,
Of the mountains where in childhood I would roam.
I have dwelt 'neath southern skies,
Where the summer never dies,
But my heart is in the mountains of my home.

I can see the little homestead on the hill;
I can hear the magic music of the rill;
There is nothing to compare,
With the love that once was there,
In that lonely little homestead on the hill.

I can see the quiet churchyard down below,
Where the mountain breezes wander to and fro,
And when God my soul will keep,
It is there I want to sleep,
With those dear old folks that loved me long ago.

FIRST GUARD. You think Old Jolly Roger's finally asleep?
SECOND GUARD. Who cares?
FIRST GUARD. Well, *I'm* ready to drop off, I can tell you. I'll pass out, if that relief aint here quick step.
SECOND GUARD. Do and you'll face a firing squad.
FIRST GUARD. Only if they prop me up to shoot. What time do you make it? *(Second Guard takes out a pocket watch and passes it in front of his eyes, without averting them from Casement.)*
SECOND GUARD. Half past three.
FIRST GUARD. Another 'alf 'our of *this?* Blimey! I'll go right round the bend. What are we lookin' at 'im for, anyway? Wot's 'e supposed to do? Sneak out a rat 'ole?
SECOND GUARD. They're afraid he'll do himself in.
FIRST GUARD. 'Ow? Scratch 'imself to death? Just watchin' 'im squirm is makin' me itch. *(His face freezes.)* Alfie…?
SECOND GUARD. What?
FIRST GUARD. 'Ow far can a louse leap?
SECOND GUARD. Dunno. Never saw a leaping louse.
FIRST GUARD. I mean a *bed* louse — like them as is suckin' 'is blood right now. 'Ow far can one o' them leap through the air?
SECOND GUARD. Dunno.
FIRST GUARD. From 'is kip clear over ta me, 'ja think?
SECOND GUARD. *(Shrugging.)* Why'd 'ja wanna know?
FIRST GUARD. 'Cause somethin' is makin' me leg itch! *(First Guard kicks off a boot to scratch one foot with the other — vigorously.)*
SECOND GUARD. No bloody louse can jump six feet!
FIRST GUARD. Is 'at right? I'll 'ave you know I saw a trained flea once what jumped clear over a bushel basket!
SECOND GUARD. Aye. But he were *trained!*

FIRST GUARD. Alfie! If a spoonfed, pampered, prima donna circus flea can jump over a bushel, don't tell me that a hungry, up-from-the-ranks, hard-nosed, Union Jack, Tower o' London louse can't leap six bloody feet! Besides, I got the bugger in my sock to prove it! *(When he bends down to scratch his ankle, First Guard spots something under Casement's cot.)*
FIRST GUARD. Alfie! Look! A rat — big as a terrier!
SECOND GUARD. Where?
FIRST GUARD. There! Right there!
SECOND GUARD. I see him! He's coming out your side! *(Second Guard snatches up his loose boot as a weapon and gets down on all fours.)* Look sharp! He knows he's trapped now. Look at them *teeth!*
FIRST GUARD. 'Is eyes is like little rubies glowin' in the dark. *Kill* 'im!
CASEMENT. No! No! Don't do that! *No* — !
FIRST GUARD. Smash the cheeky bastard! Squash 'im! *(Both Guards dive under the frail cot, arms swinging. Casement is spilled onto the floor. The dangling light bulb swings wildly, casting crazy shadows. Startled out of his sleeping nightmare into a living one, Casement lets out a wild, despairing wail, alarming the Chorus sentry outside the cell.)*
CHORUS. Quiet him down in there! You want the Guard Major up here? He'll have us all on report! *(The Guards muffle Casement's cries, right the cot, and hoist him back on it.)*
SECOND GUARD. Easy there … easy now … no 'arm done.
FIRST GUARD. You 'ad a nightmare — that's all. Rolled right off the cot in your sleep you did. 'Appens to all of us.
CASEMENT. *(Bewildered.)* Is it day or night?
FIRST GUARD. It's not yet four of the morning.
CASEMENT. Turn out that light. Please?
FIRST GUARD. You know I can't do that. Much as I'd like.
CASEMENT. For a few minutes…?
SECOND GUARD. Sorry, Gov. There ain't even a switch.
FIRST GUARD. Be a good soul, now. Put yer mind on somethin' else and maybe the bulb will *burn* out. They all do, sooner or later. *(The Guards try to hold Casement down on the cot, but he leaps up and confronts the Chorus through the cell bars. The Guards scramble after him.)*
CASEMENT. Is that rifle loaded?
CHORUS. Yes, sir.

CASEMENT. Shoot a bullet into that bulb — or my brain. I don't care which.
CHORUS. They don't allow that kind of thing in here anymore.
CASEMENT. Anymore…?
CHORUS. Oh, there was a time, sir. You wouldn't believe. In this very cell, sir. Two tiny, suckling babes — two princes of the realm they were — smothered in their sleep.
CASEMENT. That was in here…?
CHORUS. You got a very famous cell. Why, the great Sir Walter Raleigh stood on that very spot waitin' to have his head took off.
CASEMENT. *(Calming down.)* You seem to know a great deal about The Tower.
CHORUS. Thank you, sir. I read the history of it when my turn came for duty in the Guards. There was a High Chief Justice poisoned once —
CASEMENT. Don't talk of those who died. Tell me of some who lived.
CHORUS. No prisoner who ever occupied this cell … lived after.
CASEMENT. Not one…?
CHORUS. Sorry, Sir.
CASEMENT. You're Welsh, aren't you?
CHORUS. *(Delighted.)* How did you know, Sir?
CASEMENT. I heard you singing … *(The Guards draw Casement, gently, but firmly, back to the cot.)*
FIRST GUARD. 'Ear that, Taffey? 'E likes yer voice. Sing 'im another. A lullaby. Somethin' to pop 'im right off to dreamland.
CHORUS. I don't mind … if he don't. *(The Chorus sings again, softly. Casement relaxes on his cot. The Guards resume sitting on either side, staring at him. The Tower cell remains dimly visible, as bright lights come up in Attorney General Smith's office. Hall and Sir Ernley Blackwell, Legal Advisor to the Home Secretary, are with Smith, poring over statute books.)*
HALL. Ridiculous! There *has* to be a law against treason.
BLACKWELL. Not in your naval codes, Reggie. Courts-martial may not try prisoners of war. They are immune under international conventions.
SMITH. Can't he be tried as an Irish spy? That's a capital offense.
BLACKWELL. Only between sovereignties. If you're willing to grant Ireland her independence, then, perhaps —
HALL. Why not as a deserter?

BLACKWELL. A "civilian" deserter?
HALL. A civilian *defector,* then.
BLACKWELL. But he returned.
HALL. Dammit, man! He gave aid and comfort to the Krauts in their prison camps while over there!
BLACKWELL. Precisely. While he was *outside* the King's realm.
HALL. Treason is treason. Wherever it happens.
BLACKWELL. Debatable! At all events, if it happens *outside* the realm, it can only be tried at the King's Bench — a *civil* proceeding. Placing him under military custody was a tactical blunder. It confirms his status as a prisoner of war, immune to both court martial and civil prosecution.
SMITH. Well, what *are* we to do with him? Fit out another U-boat and ship him back?
BLACKWELL. Who actually signed the commitment order?
SMITH. *(Miserable.)* I'm afraid I did.
BLACKWELL. Careless, Freddy. Not like you. The Home Secretary feels it would be prudent, under the circumstances, for you to grant Sir Roger's request that he be remanded to civil custody and tried at the King's Bench.
SMITH. But he's made no such appeal…?
BLACKWELL. That is awkward. But if *I* had put him in The Tower, I'd be thinking of little else but how to get him out again, so he can be tried under the proper civil statute.
HALL. Oh, then there *is* one?
BLACKWELL. Of sorts. It was enacted in 1351 to prevent adventurers, while possessed of the Devil, from raping the queen and female members of the King's retinue.
SMITH. What does it say in plain English?
BLACKWELL. Not a word. *(Smug.)* It's written in Norman-French.
SMITH. Well, what does it say in Norman-French?
BLACKWELL. No two linguists agree. *(Smiles.)* Ideal for the purpose, don't you think?
SMITH. Has anyone ever been hanged under this remarkable law?
BLACKWELL. Not for three hundred years.
SMITH. Then what makes you think it will hang Casement?
BLACKWELL. Because *you* are Attorney General of England.
SMITH. *(Thin smile.)* I will take it as a compliment.
BLACKWELL. Please do. You may have to file its teeth to a very fine point, but you'll find the old statue has *bite* in it yet.

SMITH. We appreciate your confidence. Kindly thank the Home Secretary.
BLACKWELL. Oh, incidentally, he is *not* to emerge from his trial more popular than before. That would cause the Secretary diplomatic embarrassment with his supporters abroad.
SMITH. What am I to do about his popularity?
BLACKWELL. Whatever is required.
SMITH. The man has ardent admirers. They won't desert him over a mere trifle like treason.
HALL. *(Musing aloud.)* There are always his diaries, of course … *(Two pairs of eyes turn to stare at Hall, who casually pares his nails.)*
BLACKWELL. Diaries…?
HALL. *(Ever so casual.)* Hm? Oh, uh, his personal diaries. The ones found at his lodging in Ebery Street. There might be some entries there to dampen the ardor of his admirers.
BLACKWELL. What kind of entries?
HALL. I couldn't say … without studying them in detail.
BLACKWELL. Where are they?
SMITH. Scotland Yard. But I've gone over them already and —
BLACKWELL. How long would you need to "study" them to produce an informed opinion?
HALL. If I might have them to myself for … two weeks, say.
SMITH. Why should it take that long?
HALL. His handwriting is rather difficult.
BLACKWELL. *(Extremely careful.)* To *read,* do you mean?
HALL. *(Innocently.)* Of course … to *read* … *(They all exchange a darkly meaningful look. Blackwell smiles faintly.)*
BLACKWELL. Well, no harm in giving them a close look. Right, Freddy?
SMITH. No harm. Meanwhile, I'll have a cozy chat with Sir Roger about his present accommodations.
BLACKWELL. Good! Before he realizes your blunder.
SMITH. Coming along?
BLACKWELL. No. I have to see a man about his doggerel.
SMITH. Sorry…?
BLACKWELL. About publishing his poems.
HALL. "Poems"…?
SMITH. Coming, Reggie?
HALL. Ready, Freddy! *(As lights fade on Smith's office, he grabs his elegant cane and, followed by Hall, strides toward The Tower cell. The*

Chorus, watching them cross, picks out a ricky-ticky tune on his guitar. Infected by the music, Smith and Hall pause, look curiously at one another, then break into a softshoe routine. Lights fade up as they dance directly into Casement's cell. The Chorus, pleased with his work, smiles at the audience, then resumes his sentry post. The scene begins with the whiz-bang slap-dash pacing of a music hall skit. Smith is bubbling over with phony solicitude.)

SMITH. Good Lord, Reggie, it's true! He *is* in here! What incredible stupidity! See which donkey ordered this and have him in my office tomorrow.

HALL. That's where the donkey will be — in *your* office. *(The startled Guards draw back in deference, as Casement sits up blinking.)*

CASEMENT. You — ? Here — ?

SMITH. The wheel comes full circle, Sir Roger.

CASEMENT. But what are *you* doing here?

SMITH. The moment I learned that some blathering idiot had incarcerated you here, I came to set things right.

CASEMENT. But *you?* Of all people ... *(Abruptly, the lights dim by half and everyone freezes in a rigid tableau. After a few moments, the Chorus breaks from his pose and walks back down to the apron. He finds a spotlight, winks at the audience, then sits with his rifle across his lap to explain.)*

CHORUS. There's a fine bit of dramatic irony here, if you know what to look for. Sir Frederick Smith there used to be called "Galloper" Smith. Why? Because he used to gallop up to Ulster with illegal arms so the Protestants could fight off anybody who tried to pry them loose from England. But, Sir Roger there — him and the other rebels in the South — was all for Irish independence. When Parliament passed a new law granting independence, where did Sir Freddy "gallop" off to for more of *these? (Holds up his rifle.)* So he could shoot it off the statute books? To *Germany!* Ah, but just then — as Ireland's little war was ready to boil over ... *KA-BOOM!* The *big* war comes roaring across Belgium. And Irish independence is kicked right out the window. So, "Galloper" gets it all his own way — without having to fight. And there he stands — Attorney General of England. While Sir Roger, with independence snatched back out of his fingers, so to speak, is caught trying to sneak German arms into Ireland. The *very same thing* "Galloper" got away with. *And,* when it comes to trial, who appoints himself to prosecute Sir Roger for the very same crime he committed himself? Good old

"Galloper." *(Winks at the audience again.)* Just thought you'd like to know. As a Welshman, I have my *own* axe to grind. *(The Chorus resumes his post. Lights up full. Smith jabs the cot with his cane.)*
SMITH. The stench in here is abominable. Can't something be done about this filthy pallet?
HALL. This monstrosity should have been a museum years ago.
SMITH. *(To Guards.)* What are *you* doing in here?
FIRST GUARD. We're in 'ere to watch 'im, yer lordship.
SMITH. Watch him *what?*
FIRST GUARD. *(Shrugging.)* Whatever 'e's a mind to do, I guess.
SMITH. Appalling! Simply appalling! Notify the Guard Major. I am removing Sir Roger to a large, private, well-ventilated cell with southern exposure. *This* stinking hole is unfit for swine — let alone a distinguished knight of the realm.
HALL. You! See the Guard Major. Step lively! *(The First Guard hurries out.)*
SMITH. Bring this man some clean clothes. *Now!*
SECOND GUARD. Sir! *(He salutes and leaves.)*
SMITH. My deepest apologies, Sir Roger, for myself and for the Crown, in this disgraceful oversight. Why on earth didn't you drop me a note about these dreadful conditions?
CASEMENT. They took away my pen and paper.
SMITH. Inexcusable! You look pale, man. Here, have a brandy. *(Smith unscrews the gold knob-cup of his hollow walking-cane flask and pours.)*
CASEMENT. *(Sipping.)* Thank you.
HALL. Why didn't your solicitor lodge a protest?
CASEMENT. They won't let me see him.
SMITH. Nonsense! Even an axe murderer may see his solicitor.
CHORUS. *(Helpful.)* The gentleman calls every day. They won't show him in.
SMITH. Exasperating! Well, that's the *military* mentality for you. Once I have you in a proper *civil* prison, Sir Roger, you may rest assured that every one of your rights will receive my scrupulous attention. Right, Reggie?
HALL. I'm certain of that. Have a cigar, Sir Roger?
SMITH. And chief among them is the right to a fair and speedy trial in a *civil* court. Don't you agree, Sir Roger? *(Casement looks past them at the Chorus, who shakes his head. This causes Casement to frown, suspiciously, at the brandy cup in his one hand and cigar in the*

other. He hands them back.)
CASEMENT. No.
HALL. No?
SMITH. No?
CASEMENT. No. I prefer to die like Pearce and Connolly. Summarily court-martialed and shot.
SMITH. Be reasonable, man. We can't shoot a knight of the realm. It isn't done. Is it, Reggie?
HALL. Certainly not! What would His Majesty think?
CASEMENT. My sentry tells me that no one has ever left this cell and lived. Why should I be the first? *(Smith turns a scowl on the Chorus, who gazes at the ceiling, innocently. The Second Guard returns with clean clothes. As he puts them on, Casement recovers his courage and confidence.)* Why did you really come here?
SMITH. I've told you.
CASEMENT. Everything you've said is a lie. Let's begin with that. If you want me out of The Tower, it's for *your* good, not *mine.*
HALL. We'll chalk that up to your weakened condition.
SMITH. No, Reggie. He's right. We each want something only the other can provide. *(To Guard and Chorus.)* Leave us! *(To Chorus.) Both* of you! *(When both are gone, Smith sits on the edge of Casement's filthy cot and pats the pallet beside him, inviting Casement to sit. Casement pointedly stands facing him, instead.)* As you know, Roger, I feel nothing but contempt for your motives and your methods. But I have *never* questioned your intellect. I suggest you use it now. You've made a dreadful botch of it. The Irish Brigade … the contraband rifles … the pathetic uprising in Dublin. There's not much you can salvage. Only one thing, really.
CASEMENT. And what is that? *(Smith begins unconsciously scratching at his first few flea bites.)*
SMITH. The opportunity to present your point of view — *Ireland's* point of view — to the world at large. I could give you that chance in open court at the King's bench. But *not* in a closed court martial.
CASEMENT. What do you gain from that?
SMITH. I will prosecute for the Crown, win a celebrated treason case and see you hanged. I find all three prospects enormously appealing.
CASEMENT. *(Heartily amused.) Finally* the ring of truth. *(Reflects.)* Of course, there's always a chance I might save my life in a court-

martial.
SMITH. Don't count on it.
CASEMENT. Why not?
SMITH. Because the last appeal in *all* courts-martial is to *me* — as Attorney General of England. *(Smith is scratching with both hands by now — under his shirt — inside a sock. He frowns suddenly, glares down at the flea-infested pallet, then leaps up.)*
CASEMENT. And my last appeal in the civil courts?
HALL. Ah, *there* your chances are excellent! You could appeal all the way up to the House of Lords for a case of "exceptional public importance," like this.
SMITH. And as Crown Prosecutor, I would be obliged to see that all of your rights and prerogatives were fully protected. Anything less on my part would be seen as despicable.
CASEMENT. I will have my say?
SMITH. You have my word as a gentleman. All the customary prerogatives of open court will be at your disposal. You have only to waive your right to a court-martial. Agreed?
CASEMENT. Since I don't recognize the jurisdiction of *any* British court — civil or military — it is no great matter whether I am hanged or shot. Agreed.
SMITH. Good! That leaves only one question. As a matter of idle curiosity ... do you despise me as much as I despise you?
CASEMENT. More, I should think.
SMITH. Excellent. That will keep our gentlemen's agreement uncluttered with noble sentiments.
CASEMENT. I wasn't aware that you *had* any.
SMITH. I don't. I thought perhaps *you* did. *Reggie?*
HALL. Ready, Freddy! *(As soon as they walk away, the Chorus resumes his ricky-ticky guitar number. With Casement between them, Smith and Hall dance a fancy crossover step into the Jury Room. Jurors whistle and applaud them. There is a sudden, loud rapping on the Jury Room door. Guitar music cuts off razor-sharp. The Bailiff stalks in.)* What in the bloody 'ell is goin' on in 'ere??? *(The frolicsome Jurors are suddenly shame-faced and self-conscious.)*
READING JUROR. *Shhhhhh!*
BAILIFF. This *is* the Old Bailey! Not the bleedin' *Palladium!* I said no muckin' about! And I *meant* no muckin' about! *(Lightning flashes and thunder.) There!* Now, you've done it. We'll all 'ave to go 'ome in the rain. I 'ope you're satisfied! *(Bailiff storms out.)*

M.P. JUROR. Stick it up your jumper! *(The sound of heavy rain is heard pelting the windows. Sullivan Juror strolls to the apron and looks up at the sky. A disgruntled M.P. Juror joins him, looks up, shakes his head.)* Christ Almighty, look at 'er come. Someone up there 'as pulled the chain on us this time.

SULLIVAN JUROR. Oh, well … it's good for the farmers.

M.P. JUROR. *(Spoiling for a fight.)* Good for the farmers, is it? Now, that's a stupid thing to say. A meaningless, asinine thing to say. That's the kind of gibberish little children say, for chrissake — not grown men. Aren't you embarrassed to be caught talkin' like that?

SULLIVAN JUROR. *(Calmly.)* Not me. I'm a farmer.

SMITH JUROR. Let's have another ballot and see where we stand. *(Lights dim here as muttering Jurors start filling out ballots. Lights come up on Blackwell and Richard Morton [Casement's long-time English friend]. Morton stands nervously as the seated Blackwell leafs through a manuscript.)*

MORTON. The last two there were printed by a local poetry society, but I'm quite sure they'd give me a release.

BLACKWELL. Do sit down, Mr. Morton.

MORTON. Thank you. *(Blackwell closes the manuscript and hands it back with a thin smile.)*

BLACKWELL. I'll be candid, Mr. Morton. My associates and I don't publish verses, as a rule.

MORTON. Oh. What *is* your specialty?

BLACKWELL. Fiction. One kind or another. But you intrigue us. We might make an exception for you.

MORTON. Very kind of you.

BLACKWELL. If it were done properly on vellum with a satiny cover, say. Something tasteful for tea tables.

MORTON. I could see that, yes.

BLACKWELL. Perhaps just a *bit* of editing of the full-blooded passages?

MORTON. "Bring not the blush of shame to a young virgin's cheek." I understand, perfectly.

BLACKWELL. I expect you'd want a dedication page?

MORTON. I hadn't given that much thought.

BLACKWELL. To someone near and dear? Your *wife,* perhaps. You *are* a married man?

MORTON. Happily so — for many years. Her name is May. But I'm afraid a dedication would embarrass her.

BLACKWELL. Some early influence, then. To an admired mentor? To Roger Casement?
MORTON. *(Puzzled.)* Why him?
BLACKWELL. I understand he's an old and dear friend.
MORTON. Where did you hear that?
BLACKWELL. Isn't it true?
MORTON. I knew him … before.
BLACKWELL. Before…?
MORTON. … He went to Germany.
BLACKWELL. Was he in touch with you from there?
MORTON. *(Suspicious.)* Why do you ask?
BLACKWELL. The private writings of prominent figures make excellent reading … if they're brought out at just the right time.
MORTON. Is Roddie that famous now?
BLACKWELL. "Roddie," is it? I take it your letters from him are rather … "personal"?
MORTON. *(More suspicious.)* If it's his letters you wish to publish, shouldn't you be talking to *him?*
BLACKWELL. We are, Mr. Morton.
MORTON. What has any of this to do with my book of poems?
BLACKWELL. Nothing whatever. I am not a publisher.
MORTON. Then why did you say you were?
BLACKWELL. I didn't. I said you *intrigued* me. As, indeed, you do.
MORTON. *(Jumping up.)* Look here! I don't think this sham is a bit funny! Bringing me here under false —
BLACKWELL. Why did Sir Roger assume *your* name when he was arrested?
MORTON. I didn't know he had.
BLACKWELL. There are several things you don't know about "Dear Old Roddie." I think you had better sit down, Mr. Morton.
MORTON. I'm not staying!
BLACKWELL. Sit down, Mr. Morton!
MORTON. Who are you, really?
BLACKWELL. Ernley Blackwell, Legal Advisor to the Home Secretary.
MORTON. I won't tell you anything that can be used against him.
BLACKWELL. On the contrary, you've told me a great deal. You confirm that he went to Germany. That he kept up a clandestine correspondence while there. And that "Dear Roddie's" personal letters are too intimate to publish. We're making excellent progress,

Mr. Morton. Do sit down. *(Morton sags back into the chair, intimidated. Blackwell takes folded pages out of his pocket and offers them.)*
MORTON. What's this?
BLACKWELL. Something we *do* intend to bring out for a few discriminating readers, like yourself. Entries from his personal diary. *(Morton reads a moment then looks up, appalled, at Blackwell's impassive face. As Morton resumes reading, lights fade here and come up full in the jury room, where the ballots have been counted. It is still raining.)*
READING JUROR. We *still* don't have a verdict. There are *two* for acquittal.
M.P. JUROR. Well, we all know who one is ... *(Scowls at Casement Juror.)* but 'oo's the *other* bleedin' 'eart in this lot? 'Ave we got another Irishman in 'ere, passin' 'imself off fer English?
CASEMENT JUROR. Sir Roger never claimed to be anything but Irish. Even in the Consular service he made up his own letterhead: "Consulate for the English Empire and the Irish Republic."
RYAN JUROR. He didn't?
CASEMENT JUROR. Until the Foreign Office called him on the carpet.
RYAN JUROR. Did he change it, then?
CASEMENT JUROR. Yes. "Consul to the British Crown and the Irish Crown of Thorns."
ROBINSON JUROR. God bless the cheeky bloke. *Best* thing I've heard about him.
READING JUROR. It doesn't forgive him going over to the Huns.
CASEMENT JUROR. He never went over to them.
READING JUROR. I mean to the prison camps. Talking to Irish boys. What was he there for, if not treason?
CASEMENT JUROR. Irish independence!
READING JUROR. That *is* treason — in time o' war! *(Another lightning flash and thunderclap. Jurors hunch down in their jackets shove their hands in their pockets and shuffle along, as if in the open rain. As lights cross-fade to Limburg prisoner-of-war camp, the Chorus strums the opening strains of "Long Way to Tipperary." The glum Prisoners begin whistling along with the guitar. When all of them are whistling, the Chorus stops playing. Casement appears with an armed German Guard on an upper level and addresses them with intense conviction.)*
CASEMENT. All of you here — every last Irishman — was cap-

tured while risking your life for Belgium. And why? Because it was in England's interest to send you there! Are you willing to do as much for your own country? To free Ireland?
NEILL. I heard that your "Irish Brigade" won't fight for Ireland, at all. The Huns want us to drive the British out of Egypt!
CASEMENT. That rumor is utterly false! The Irish-German Treaty is explicit on that very point. *(Pulls out a paper.)* Listen! "Article Two: The Irish Brigade shall fight *solely* in the cause of Ireland. Under *no* circumstances shall it fight for Germany."
NEILL. Maybe that's how it reads —
CASEMENT. It does! Look!
NEILL. And *maybe* the Chancellor signed it —
CASEMENT. With his seal of office! See for yourself!
NEILL. And *maybe* the rotten horse meat stew they feed us here is really choice cut tenderloin! *(Casement jumps down and waves the Treaty in Neill's face.)*
CASEMENT. Don't you believe the evidence of your own eyes, Soldier?
NEILL. I *used* to! When I still *had* eyes! *(Groping in space, Neill sweeps aside the Treaty, grabs Casement's lapel, snarling.)* That was before the Chancellor and me — we made our own private "treaty" — with a potato masher!
CASEMENT. I'm sorry, Corporal … I didn't know —
NEILL. Never mind that! I see *some* things better without eyes! Like you, f'instance. I see right through you to the empty 'ole where a man's guts should be! You traitorous, cowardly — ! *(Neill grabs Casement's throat and tries to throttle him. The German Guard drags him away. Casement recovers his composure and tries to continue, but the Prisoners aren't impressed. As he speaks, several disdainfully turn their backs on him.)*
CASEMENT. You see what the British did to the mind of this brave, young Irishman by sending him into the trenches to fight for tyranny! No man wants to lose his lifeblood — nor his sight. But how much better to lose them fighting for Ireland!
ROBINSON. I have given all the blood I can spare, thank you.
CASEMENT. If you have no appetite for freedom — no love left for your homeland — then God save Ireland.
ROBINSON. Aye! God save Ireland … from *traitors! (The German Guard puts his bayonet to Robinson's throat and looks to Casement for orders. Other Prisoners close in around the Guard,*

threateningly. Robinson defiantly starts whistling "Tipperary" again. Others join in.)

CASEMENT. Think what you like of *me!* But remember Ireland! She *needs* you! *All* of you! I'll leave the enlistment book here for a few days. I expect to see at least a hundred names in it!

ROBINSON. A *hundred?* Sure, why not a *thousand?* Why pester us when you got the Kaiser's whole, bleedin', sausage-stuffed army on your side? Enlist *them* to fight for Ireland! Not broken-down skeletons the likes of us that's already had a bellyful of fightin' I can tell you. *(The German Guard threatens with his bayonet again. Casement waves him off. The Prisoners show their contempt by walking away from Casement, still whistling. The rain fades out. Lights come up in the holding cell at the Old Bailey where Casement is lying on his cot. Another young Sentry [the Chorus] whispers through the bars.)*

CHORUS. Pssst! Sir Roger! *(Casement goes to the Chorus, who glances around before passing him a letter.)*

CHORUS. I didn't give you this.

CASEMENT. Of course not. Thank you.

CHORUS. *(Innocently.)* For *what,* sir? *(Smiling.)* God bless. *(Casement opens the sealed letter. As he reads it with growing interest, a pool of light picks up Gertrude at her desk reading aloud what she has written.)*

GERTRUDE. "Dearest cousin … If you are reading this, you know that you have friends … even in that beastly place. However badly they treat you, you mustn't let them break your spirit. A fine Irish barrister — one of the very best — is coming over to take charge of your defence. And a leading authority on parliamentary law is donating his services on your behalf. Bernard Shaw's wife, Charlotte, made a generous contribution. And Bernard, himself, offered to write your closing appeal to the jury … if you wish it … As you must know by now, the uprising in Dublin over Easter week was crushed. Many lives were lost … but some good has come of it. Public resentment over British mistreatment of Ireland — and of *you* — is rising daily … here and abroad. *(She puts down the letter and goes closer to the cell to watch him as she recites the rest of it.)* Oh, Roger, I must tell you something else that happened at the Dublin Post Office during the pitched battle on Monday. It illustrates why the Irish can be beaten down, but never — ever — conquered. Pearse and the other republicans were pinned down inside the building under a steady stream of gunfire from soldiers in the street and sharpshooters in Trinity Tower.

About one in the afternoon they looked up in horror and disbelief as a little, elderly lady walked right in the front door with a small parcel. The postal clerk had fled, so she entered his cage, weighed her parcel, rummaged in her purse for the right change and left it on the counter.

With British bullets ricocheting all around her, she dropped her parcel in the "overseas bin" and left. Outside, she felt a few drops of rain, so she put up her umbrella to ward them off and walked on home, calm as you please. *(Casement chuckles over the letter. Gertrude is pleased and leaves. The Chorus alerts him.)*

CHORUS. Pssst! A chaplin is coming, Sir Roger! *(Casement hides the letter. Father Ryan approaches, hesitantly.)*

RYAN. Good morning, Sir Roger.

CASEMENT. Father Ryan?

RYAN. I told them it would anger you. But they insisted it was me — or no one. Shall I leave? *(Casement's features soften. He goes to Father Ryan and shakes his hand warmly. The Chorus leaves them alone.)*

CASEMENT. Please stay, Father.

RYAN. I beg your forgiveness.

CASEMENT. No, I beg yours. I had no right to ask you to betray your oath. You did what you had to. *(Wan smile.)* So did I.

RYAN. Don't despair. You have a very skilled advocate in Sergeant Sullivan. He may well get you acquitted.

CASEMENT. No. They couldn't justify executing Pearse and Connolly, if they let me off. I'll be convicted and hanged, Father.

RYAN. If you're reconciled, Roger, why did you send for a priest?

CASEMENT. I was baptized a Catholic. But when I went "British," I went all the way — clear to the Church of England. I wish to be reconciled with Rome before I am hanged.

RYAN. I see. You're sure this is a profound conviction? And not an act of desperation?

CASEMENT. *(Smiling.)* Do I seem desperate, Father? I wish to die in the faith. And be buried in holy ground.

RYAN. Do you believe in the Only Redeemer, Our Lord, Jesus Christ?

CASEMENT. I do.

RYAN. Do you believe in the Holy Trinity, the Communion of Saints, and in Mary, the Holy Virgin, Mother of God?

CASEMENT. I do, Father.

RYAN. Praise God, for *one* blessing out of all this grief. I'll go to the Cardinal at once for a Faculty of Reconciliation.
CASEMENT. Thank you, Father. *(Ryan starts out, then hesitates.)*
RYAN. He will ask if you forgive your enemies.
CASEMENT. I do.
RYAN. *All* of them, Roger. Even Sir Frederick Smith…?
CASEMENT. Poor Freddy. Yes, even him.
RYAN. Despite all they've done against you? Even the use of your diary? *(A subtle, dark, apprehension comes over Casement's face.)*
CASEMENT. My diary…?
RYAN. There can be no mental reservations, Roger. You cannot deceive God.
CASEMENT. What use have they made of my diary?
RYAN. You weren't told?
CASEMENT. Tell me now.
RYAN. *(Sudden decision.)* No. Your soul is composed. God forbid I trouble it anew. I'll see Cardinal Bourne at once.
CASEMENT. Wait! Father Ryan!
RYAN. Take it to prayer, Roger. The only true comfort is there.
CASEMENT. But Father — ? *(Ryan is gone. The Chorus resumes his post outside the cell.)* What's your name, son?
CHORUS. Me, Sir? Billy, Sir.
CASEMENT. Have you heard something about my diary, Billy? *(The Chorus looks at the audience.)*
CHORUS. Your … "diary," Sir?
CASEMENT. You *have,* Billy! I see it in your eyes! You know something!
CHORUS. I — I — I don't know what you mean, sir.
CASEMENT. They've used my diary against me. But *how,* Billy? *How?*
CHORUS. I can't be seen talking to you, sir.
CASEMENT. *Dear God!* Does *everyone* know — except *me? (A signal bell rings three times.)*
CHORUS. They're calling for you up in the courtroom, sir. Time to go back in the dock. Sorry, sir. *(Lights transpose to the Old Bailey courtroom. As the Chorus escorts Casement to the dock, Robinson takes the stand.)*
SMITH. Now, Private Robinson, would you tell the jury how many prisoners at Limburg joined Sir Roger's treasonous brigade?
ROBINSON. Not many.

SMITH. Ten or a dozen?
ROBINSON. Two or three.
SMITH. Were you one of those?
ROBINSON. Sir?
SMITH. Did you join his so-called "Irish Brigade"?
ROBINSON. No, Sir. If I'd signed on with *him,* I wouldn't be up here giving *your* version, now would I? *(The ripple of laughter that tends to discredit Robinson's testimony irks Smith. Reading gavels for silence.)*
SMITH. Let's clear up *that* point, Private Robinson. Has anyone for the Crown suggested that you will receive preferential treatment in exchange for your testimony?
ROBINSON. Sir?
SMITH. I'm asking if you were *bribed!*
ROBINSON. I don't want to be a private forever, do I, sir?
SMITH. Were you *promised* a *promotion?*
ROBINSON. *(Ever so wise.)* Promised? Oh, no, sir. I'll just have to take my chances on that score. And hope for the best. *(Robinson's broad wink to Smith prompts cynical chuckles around the courtroom.)*
READING. Let's have dignity at the King's Bench. Proceed, Sir Frederick.
SMITH. *(Extreme patience.)* Now, then, Private Robinson …
ROBINSON. Yes, Sir! Right, Sir! I've got it all straight now, Sir! *(Smith contemplates Robinson's egregious grin and decides not to risk it.)*
SMITH. Oh, never mind. You may cross-examine, Mr. Sullivan. *(Alexander Sullivan, Sergeant of the Irish Bar, has great dignity. His convoluted speech and deferential manner are not affectations. He knows no other way.)*
SULLIVAN. I am very much indebted to the honorable gentleman.
SMITH. Not at all.
SULLIVAN. Your Lordship, if, as I comprehend it, this man's testimony was designed to prove what Sir Roger may — or may not — have done on a given day, in a given place, within the German Empire, then, I respectfully submit, it is the right of the defence not merely to cross examine this particular witness, but also to have license to commission an advocate of our own to the German Empire to solicit counter-witnesses.
READING. It is not within this court's power to grant that license, Mr. Sullivan. We are at war with the German Empire.
SULLIVAN. Anticipating that, Your Lordship, I arranged for the

assistance of an attorney from Philadelphia. As the United States are not at war with the German Empire, I commissioned him to Germany where he took sworn affidavits and waits now in Switzerland for authorization to bring them here.

READING. Have you applied to the government for a border permit?

SULLIVAN. I have, Your Lordship.

READING. With what result?

SULLIVAN. I am informed that no one who went to Limburg for that purpose will be admitted to this country.

READING. Who handed down this ruling?

SMITH. *(Rises to explain.)* I did, Your Lordship. Not as the Crown Prosecutor, of course. But in my separate capacity as Attorney General. It involves national security, about which I am not free to say more. *(He starts to sit, then adds:)* Allow me to assure the court, however, that there is no conflict of interest here.

SULLIVAN. Nonetheless, Your Lordship, he has his testimony and we do not. I move that either his be stricken, or ours allowed.

SMITH. Speaking now as Crown Prosecutor, I strongly object to that on the grounds that *any* testimony supplied to this court by an enemy of England, would be suspect of perjury *prima facie.*

SULLIVAN. Then, surely, Private Robinson's testimony is equally suspect on the converse ground that he has become a *friend* of England.

READING. Mr. Sullivan, there is no evidence to suggest that the witness has perjured himself.

SULLIVAN. Because my learned adversary prevents me from obtaining such evidence.

READING. *(Pointedly.)* Let me understand you perfectly, Mr. Sullivan. Are you asking this court to entertain the suspicion that the Counsel for the Crown has, in some way, exercised his various prerogatives to bestow on himself an unfair advantage?

SULLIVAN. I may have flirted with that very suspicion, Your Lordship.

READING. Then you *do* enjoin us here in open court, beyond the immunity of chamber conference, to imagine such a *libelous* thing?

SULLIVAN. *(Beaten and knows it.)* Your Lordship will accept my fullest submission on the point. I withdraw my hasty and ill-considered motion.

READING. With apologies, I should think?
SULLIVAN. With the most respectful apologies to my learned friend for any possible exception he may have taken to the thoughtless phrasing of my remarks.
SMITH. *(Faint smile.)* None taken.
READING. The court accepts the competence of this witness. You may question him, Mr. Sullivan.
SULLIVAN. No questions, Your Lordship.
READING. In that event, as it is now half past five, we shall adjourn until ten o'clock tomorrow morning to resume the prosecution. *(Others stand until Reading exits, then drift away in hushed conversation until only Smith and Sullivan are left collecting briefs into their satchels. Smith looks sidelong at Sullivan, weighing something, then crosses to him and holds out a large brown envelope. Sullivan looks at it but doesn't take it.)*
SULLIVAN. What is it?
SMITH. Photographic copies of pages from Sir Roger's private diaries.
SULLIVAN. Why give them to me?
SMITH. Don't look so wary, Alex. It's a friendly offering. Your American attorney being stuck in Switzerland is a setback for you. This will even things up.
SULLIVAN. If it's relevant, why isn't it in evidence?
SMITH. You'll know when you read it.
SULLIVAN. I'll know when you put it in evidence.
SMITH. Don't be stuffy, Alex. It could save his life.
SULLIVAN. At what cost?
SMITH. After reading this, if you enter a motion to change his plea to "guilty, but insane," I won't object.
SULLIVAN. That aspersion won't make you very popular at Buckingham.
SMITH. What aspersion?
SULLIVAN. That His Majesty confers knighthoods on crackpots.
SMITH. Your first obligation to your client is to save his life.
SULLIVAN. There is no question of our pleading insanity. Good day.
SMITH. I offer this as an act of fairness. Do you fling it in my face?
SULLIVAN. It is an act of blackmail. Nothing more. You think you have discovered some odious flaw in Sir Roger's character. But it has no bearing on treason or you'd have put it in evidence. You

want me to know it's there — hanging over my head. If I dare to call character witnesses, then your insidious, skulking discovery will be relevant. Well, you have misjudged me and my strategy. I am calling *no* witnesses for the defence. Not even Sir Roger!

SMITH. Yes, I know. You plan to let him make a statement *not* under oath, which I cannot cross examine. Then you will deliver an impassioned closing address to sway the jury to acquittal.

SULLIVAN. *(Astonished.)* How did you guess *that?*

SMITH. My dear fellow, this trial is far too important for guesswork. I *read* it in your private correspondence with the prisoner.

SULLIVAN. That correspondence is *privileged!*

SMITH. So I've heard.

SULLIVAN. That is the most *appalling* confession I have ever heard from the mouth of a government official.

SMITH. You have lived a rather sheltered life … in Ireland.

SULLIVAN. Why are you telling me this?

SMITH. So you will read his diary.

SULLIVAN. I will *not* read it!

SMITH. You intend to stick to your plan, then? To send the jury out with your stirring appeal to mercy and fair play ringing in their ears?

SULLIVAN. I do.

SMITH. And you really think it will sway them to an acquittal?

SULLIVAN. I have every expectation.

SMITH. Hm … it's just possible. *(Crisply.)* So, *I* will make the closing appeal.

SULLIVAN. You cannot!

SMITH. Indeed, I can. That is my unique privilege, as ranking law officer of England.

SULLIVAN. But I am entitled to it by long custom and legal tradition.

SMITH. True. But I am entitled to pre-empt you by the letter of British law — a prerogative you are surely aware of?

SULLIVAN. Yes. But it is as obsolete as the rack and the thumbscrew. It has passed from civilized usage!

SMITH. I shall revive it.

SULLIVAN. *(Outraged.)* Am I to have no options whatever? *(Smith holds out the brown envelope again. Sullivan trembles with rage.)* I have spent forty years of my life before the bar. Forty years of dedication to the belief that man has ascended from the swamps and the jungles to the world's highest parliaments through the rule of law. It is a profound disappointment and a deep, personal loss to see that, after all these millennia, a man may yet rise to be "ranking law officer of England," with one foot still firmly planted in *primeval slime! (Sullivan whirls abruptly and stalks out. Smith is still smarting from the insult, when Hall materializes beside him, holding out his hand for the envelope. Smith hesitates, then gives it to him.)*

SMITH. Very well, Reggie ... *your* way. *(Smith exits. Hall smiles after him, then crosses briskly to another area where several Press Officials await him.)*

HALL. Sorry to keep you, Gentlemen. I know you all have deadlines. But I think you'll agree this was worth waiting for. *(Hall passes out photocopies. Some frown, others smile, as they smell good copy.)*

AMERICAN REPORTER. I don't know British law, Captain. But I could never publish *this* in a New York paper.

HALL. No, I didn't imagine you could, Mr. Sweet. But you might convey it to your editor. In view of the obscene practices not merely recorded here, but extolled in *rhapsodical* detail, the *New York Sun*'s efforts to elevate Sir Roger to sainthood seem to us decidedly premature.

AMERICAN REPORTER. *(Still reading.)* To say the least ...

HALL. Mr. Shorter, I might say the same of our own *Daily Sphere.*

SHORTER. I thought he was on trial for treason. Will these be used in court?

HALL. No. His private morals are not the issue.

SHORTER. I agree with that — absolutely. *(Shorter hands back his copy and leaves. Hall distributes more.)*

HALL. Mr. Allen ... Mr. Donald ... Mr. McColl ...

ALLEN. Captain Hall.

HALL. Yes, Mr. Allen?

ALLEN. Has Sir Roger seen any of this?

HALL. Seen it? He *wrote* it.

ALLEN. Has he admitted that?

HALL. His handwriting has been officially confirmed.

ALLEN. By whom?

HALL. Handwriting experts from the Department of Naval Intelligence.

ALLEN. By that you mean expert forgers?

HALL. *(Icy.)* I mean experts *on* forgeries.

ALLEN. *Government* experts?
HALL. Yes. Certainly.
ALLEN. I couldn't put any of this on the Associated Press wire without showing it to Sir Roger first — to confirm or deny.
HALL. I'm afraid not. No one may see him 'til after the trial.
ALLEN. Then the AP will consider this … after the trial.
HALL. It may not be newsworthy then.
ALLEN. Is it now? *(Allen hands back his copy and leaves.)*
HALL. I'm afraid America has never fully recovered from the puritanical visitation of the *Mayflower.* Naturally, gentlemen, you will have to be particular to whom you show these. But the government are confident that — as *worldly* representatives of the Fourth Estate — you will know how to disseminate these. In doing so, you will perform a patriotic service to His Majesty's government. In this hour of national peril, England counts on every man to do his duty. *(The Chorus to one side, takes up his guitar and begins strumming a soul-stirring version of "Pomp and Circumstance." During the above pomposity, Hall and Press Officials have been soberly folding the photocopies into paper airplanes.)* I see you stand like greyhounds in the slips, straining upon the start. The game's afoot! Follow your spirit, and upon this charge, cry "God for Harry, England and Saint George!" *(At Hall's prompting they all advance to the apron and begin sailing their paper airplanes, willy-nilly out into the audience.)*
PRESS OFFICIALS. *(In unison.)* God for Harry! … England! … and Saint George! *(The Chorus switches to a rollicking Elizabethan madrigal that inspires Press Officials to prance about on their toes. As they continue sailing paper airplanes at each other, lights cross-fade with them into the jury room. When they are fully caught up in this grotesquerie, whopping and ducking thrown planes, the Bailiff storms into the room, aghast at what he sees.)*
BAILIFF. 'Ere, now! Didn't I say *no muckin' about? (The Jurors freeze, as paper planes continue to glide down around them. The Chorus stops playing and turns to the audience with an innocent "Who, me?" shrug. Blackout.)*

End of Act One

ACT TWO

Action is continuous from Act One. The shame-faced Jurors are still frozen in place. The indignant Bailiff's eyes follow the flight of one last wayward airplane, as it circles down from the flies.

BAILIFF. *Well?* I 'ope you ain't waitin' fer *me* to pick 'em up! *(The embarrassed Jurors quickly gather up the planes and stuff them in a wastebasket, as the Bailiff gives them a piece of his mind.)* Goin' on nineteen years now … day in … day out. Home to the missus every night. *(Mimics.)* "What's new at the Old Bailey, luv?" says she. Same bloody question, night after night. "What's new at the Old Bailey, luv?" After a while I got to makin' up stories. Just to keep 'er 'appy, you know? "Well, Luv," says I, "I caught a three-foot shark today swimmin' about in the public loo." "Nooo???" says she. "Wot didja use for bait, then?"

So, I give that up. I tried sneakin' in. Shoes off. Tiptoe ever so quiet up the stairs. Ease into the bedroom and — "Hello, luv. What's new at the Old Bailey?" Blimey!

But tonight I finally 'ave somethin' to tell 'er, aint I? I don't understand it, gents. You got plenty o' time to play with paper gliders. But there's so many *pantywaists* 'ere, ya can't find time to 'ang one bleedin' *butterfly! (Bailiff wheels in disgust and storms out of the jury room.)*

M.P. JUROR. *(To Casement Juror.)* It's *you* he's talkin' about!

CASEMENT JUROR. Oh, is it?

M.P. JUROR. Yer the one what won't admit what Old Jolly Roger really is.

CASEMENT JUROR. Which is?

M.P. JUROR. A *pervert!* A twisted-up, sucked-dry, burnt-out case! Do you want 'im loose on the street, for chrissake?

CASEMENT JUROR. I worry *more* about the likes of *you* on the loose.

M.P. JUROR. 'Ere now, Gov! You tyke that back, or I'll —

CASEMENT JUROR. Frankly, I don't care a damn what the man

is in private. It's nobody's business *what* he is with his pants down. In public, he's a bloody *giant!* A better man than any here.

M.P. JUROR. Speak for yourself! I've 'alf a mind to split yer face open for a crack like that! *(Sullivan Juror steps between them, allowing Casement Juror to retreat.)*

SULLIVAN JUROR. He's got the same right to an opinion as anyone.

M.P. JUROR. 'Oo asked *you?*

SULLIVAN JUROR. No one. That's *my* opinion. *(M.P. Juror bristles, then shrugs and walks away, disgusted. Blackwell Juror approaches Sullivan Juror.)*

BLACKWELL JUROR. It really doesn't affect you? What Sir Roger is?

SULLIVAN JUROR. Not one iota.

BLACKWELL JUROR. Someone like that doesn't make your skin crawl? Even a little?

SULLIVAN JUROR. It's not relevant.

BLACKWELL JUROR. Of course, not. It's *chemical!* Do you really feel no aversion imaging Sir Roger with those native boys? Those young sailors? Naked together? Touching? Exploring? *(Blackwell Juror's hands wander over Sullivan Juror, making him suddenly bolt away. Blackwell Juror laughs, cynically.)*

SULLIVAN JUROR. All right! What does that prove?

BLACKWELL JUROR. That you may not be as high-minded as you let on.

SULLIVAN JUROR. Perversion is *not* a capital offence! The charge is *treason!* And they failed to prove it.

SMITH JUROR. *Prove* it? The man *admits* it! He *gloats* over it!

SULLIVAN JUROR. Even so, the law is ambiguous. The Treason Statute does not say exactly —

M.P. JUROR. Aw, you ain't gonna drag out that technicality again, are you? *(Disgusted Jurors, tired of hearing about this, walk away from Sullivan Juror, toward the courtroom.)*

SULLIVAN JUROR. The law is nothing *but* a collection of technicalities. It's absolutely germane to know if Sir Roger was tried under a proper statute.

READING JUROR. But how are we to establish that?

SULLIVAN JUROR. There is only one way to be certain … *(Eager to make his case with the other Jurors, he pursues them into the courtroom, as the lights cross-fade there.)*

SULLIVAN. ... And that is to examine the original parchment document from the Records Office. Pending its arrival, Your Lordship, my learned friend and expert on Parliamentary law, Professor John Morgan, has prepared a brief on the antecedent interpretations of the Treason Statue for the Court's guidance.
MORGAN. *(Reading.)* "Your Lordship, learned counsel for the Crown, gentlemen of the jury, you have before you — "
SMITH. One moment, please. I am obliged to point out a difficulty here, Milord. The prisoner already *has* the two counsel allotted to him by law — my distinguished adversary, Mr. Sullivan, and his able second, Mr. Jones. Professor Morgan makes a *third.*
SULLIVAN. His scholarly analysis is fundamental to our defence, Milord.
READING. The law is quite clear on this point, Mr. Sullivan. *(Sullivan motions Jones to take over, while he dives into a statute book.)*
JONES. Milord, the Crown prosecutor has on hand no less an authority than Sir Ernley Blackwell, Advisor to the Home Secretary. *(Morgan indicates Blackwell sitting nearby. Blackwell smiles and nods.)*
READING. Yes. The law is quite clear on that point, as well.
JONES. *(Needling.)* If the Attorney General feels that his present overwhelming advantage is inadequate, I am prepared to withdraw as second counsel to make way for Professor Morgan. *(Reading looks to Smith, who stares, scornfully, at Jones, then shrugs.)*
READING. There is no need to withdraw. We will hear Professor Morgan as *amicus curiae.*
MORGAN. "Your Lordship, learned counsel for the Crown — " *(He is interrupted again as a large, yellow-tinted glass case is carried in by two Guards and placed on the exhibits table. Second Guard is the Chorus.)*
SULLIVAN. A moment, Professor. This must be the Treason Statute of 1351. *(The Chorus holds up a hand for silence, then repositions the case in the precise spot to catch the only shaft of direct sunlight slanting into the room. He gives the audience a "How's that? Better?" grin, then snaps to attention. The First Guard draws a thermometer from a slot in the case.)*
FIRST GUARD. Nineteen-point-three centigrade!
CHORUS. Nineteen-point-three! Check! *(First Guard shakes down the thermometer and reinserts it into the case, while the Chorus records it on a clipboard.)*

FIRST GUARD. Humidity: Sixty-eight-point-eight percent.
CHORUS. Sixty-eight-point-eight. Check!
FIRST GUARD. Better make it quick, Your Lordship. She's slipping fast.
READING. What happens to it?
FIRST GUARD. This parchment is more than five and a half centuries old. We can't keep it away from the controlled environment of the records vault for long — even in this special transport case.
SULLIVAN. How do I take it out?
FIRST GUARD. Take it *out?* You can't. She's hermetically sealed. Do you want a priceless pillar of English law to flake off and crumble to dust in your hands?
SULLIVAN. Terribly sorry. I didn't know.
FIRST GUARD. He wants to take it out. You ever heard the like?
CHORUS. Vandalism! He can read it through the glass — or not at all.
SULLIVAN. May I use a magnifier, then?
FIRST GUARD. Magnifier? Check that, Bob.
CHORUS. Right! *(Checks his clipboard.)* Hummm … "maggots" … "Magna Charta" … Here it is, "magnifier." Allowed! *(Sullivan takes out a jeweler's loupe, fits it to his eye, stares into the case, then looks up, triumphant.)*
SULLIVAN. Just as I thought. I move to quash the indictment.
READING. On what possible ground, Mr. Sullivan?
SULLIVAN. The indictment is defective. It cites no offense known to the law.
MORGAN. That is precisely the burden of my brief, if you will permit —
SULLIVAN. Patience, my learned friend. May it please the court, the indictment, as drawn, charges that Sir Roger *(Reads.)* "… did traitorously give aid and comfort to an enemy of England in parts beyond the seas, to wit, the Empire of Germany." But, Milord, there is, in this venerable statute, no such crime as committing treason *outside* the realm.
SMITH. Utter nonsense! The indictment was drawn up from that very statute, Milord — word for word!
READING. Is it valid, then?
SULLIVAN and SMITH. Yes, most certainly!
No, definitely not!
READING. *(Long-suffering.)* All right, Mr. Sullivan, put your case.

SULLIVAN. The statute, as you well know, dates from the reign of Edward III and is written in Norman French. The customary English translation reads, "If a man be adherent to the enemies of our Lord the King *in his realm,* bringing them aid and comfort *in his realm,* or elsewhere, he shall be guilty," et cetera.
SMITH. Well? What's wrong with that? *"Elsewhere,"* it says. Germany is elsewhere, is it not?
SULLIVAN. But the actual word in Norman French is *"par alilleurs,"* which may, indeed, mean "elsewhere." But it may also mean "otherwise." That is to say, "in some other manner." I submit that the proper reading of the phrase is "... bringing them aid and comfort in his realm in some other manner."
SMITH. Really, Milord! With that interpretation ... *(With an impatient wave of his hand, the Chorus silences the attorneys, who freeze. He walks to the apron to reassure the audience.)*
CHORUS. When all is said and done, the printed transcript of this trial will cover *three hundred* pages — with print *that* small. And *most* of those pages will be the very thing they're quibbling over right now — does the Statue apply to what Sir Roger done? Or not?

Well, there's no need you squirming in your seats through all that when I can say what's what in language a good deal plainer than Norman-French!

All attorneys love to quibble over the *letter* of the law. But here's *worse!* They're niggling over a *comma* between letters. The gist of it is this — there's two ways to translate this statute into English. One way makes — *(Stops himself.)* But why was an English law written in Norman-French in the first place? Because Edward III wasn't content with England. He wanted France, as well. After two invasions failed miserably, he decided to call himself King of France, anyway. That amused the French. But you know how prickly the frogs are over their precious language. When Edward tried to steal that, too, it started the Hundred Years War. *(Stops himself again.)* But that's another story. I was saying, there's two ways to translate the statute from slippery French into plain-speaking English. One way makes Sir Roger a free man. The other makes him a traitor — but *only* if there's a comma where a comma needs to be. That's what all this fuss is about. And it'll go on forever, if I don't do something. *(The Chorus walks back up to the parchment case, takes the loupe out of Sullivan's eye, and plants it in Morgan's eye.*

Smith brings out his own Sherlockian magnifying glass, which makes one eye appear grotesquely large when he looks through it. As soon as the Chorus takes his post, court action resumes.)

SULLIVAN. For the customary English translation to be meaningful requires that the entire phrase "bringing them aid and comfort in his realm" be set off with a comma. I submit, your Lordship, that no comma exists on this parchment.

SMITH. There is a comma! It's as plain as the nose on your face.

SULLIVAN. Where?

SMITH. Right there! Just right of the curlicue on the tail of the "m." You see it?

SULLIVAN. There is no comma, Your Lordship.

SMITH. Of course it's a comma. That mark on the parchment *must* be a comma, Milord. The statute is meaningless without a comma there!

SULLIVAN. After five and a half centuries, it's too late to invest this document with meaning. *Or* punctuation! *(Morgan is hunched over the case, engrossed.)*

READING. Professor Morgan?

MORGAN. In my considered opinion, it is a fly-speck, Milord.

READING. Fly-speck? What's a fly-speck?

MORGAN. The turd of a fly, Milord.

READING. *(Outraged.)* On an *Act of Parliament — ???*

FIRST GUARD. *(Clucks his tongue.)* The case is hermetically sealed, too.

CHORUS. Cunning little bugger. *(To audience.)* How do you suppose he did it? *(Reading comes down from the bench to see for himself. The case is hidden in the huddle of bodies.)*

SMITH. All right! All right! There's no comma. But the phrase is clearly set off by brackets.

SULLIVAN. Brackets were not *invented* until the eighteenth century.

FIRST GUARD. Nineteen-point-two centigrade!

MORGAN. When do I get to read my brief?

CHORUS. Nineteen-point-two. Check!

SULLIVAN. I rest my motion to quash, Your Lordship.

FIRST GUARD. Humidity: sixty-four flat!

READING. Put the Crown's rebuttal, Mr. Smith.

CHORUS. Sixty-four flat? That's into the danger zone. Sharp eye now.

FIRST GUARD. Right, Bob!

MORGAN. "Your Lordship, learned counsel for the Crown, gentlemen of the jury, you have before you — "
READING. I said Mr. Smith's rebuttal!
MORGAN. But I was here first!
READING. Nevertheless —
MORGAN. I worked seven weeks without fee to prepare this brief!
READING. You are not a leading counsel.
MORGAN. I am a leading authority on Parliamentary Law!
READING. Either you sit in peace — or you stand in contempt!
(Morgan weighs this, than sits, pouting.)
SMITH. With the court's indulgence I must say that this scurrilous attack upon one of the oldest bulwarks of British law is not only shocking, but — *Professor!!! (In a petty pique, Morgan has snatched a heavy law book and raised it in both hands over the fragile glass case, ready to smash it to smithereens. He freezes there, trembling on the razor's edge of violence. The Guards inch toward him.)*
MORGAN. Stay back! Take one more step and I'll do it!
READING. Here, now! Return that book at once!
MORGAN. If *anyone* makes a sudden move, I'll *kill* it!
SULLIVAN. Professor Morgan, what can you possibly expect to achieve by this rash behavior? *(A thin, maniacal smile passes over Morgan's face. He glances at his brief.)*
MORGAN. "Your Lordship, learned counsel for the Crown, gentlemen of the jury, you have before you one of the most baffling — STAY WHERE YOU ARE! — legal questions in the entire canon of civil law. Here is an ancient statute encrusted with a modern interpretation by Lord Coke which is, itself, over three hundred and fifty years old. And even Lord Coke did not boggle at blotting out an entire phrase to make his interpretation wash. *(Sniffs the air and goes on.)* His initial rape of the statute was buttressed in turn by Hale, Hawkins, Fitzherbert — *(Sniffs again.)* I say, is something burning? *(A thin wisp of smoke has been curling up from the glass case under Morgan's nose — unnoticed by those staring at the book.)*
FIRST GUARD. *(Panic.)* It's the parchment! Who left this magnifier on the case? *(To Smith.) You!* You focused sunlight on her, you silly jackass!
SMITH. Terribly sorry … I didn't realize …
FIRST GUARD. Shut up! And stand back! Give her room! *(Even Morgan is caught up in this crisis and forgets himself. British to the core, they instantly form a human fire-brigade down the length of the*

exhibits table. Reading snatches up his water pitcher and fills a glass. It is passed down — hand to hand — to the Chorus. He grins at the audience, as he opens the case, dumps in the water and passes back the empty glass for a refill. And another. Over the babble of excited voices, the Chorus begins to whistle "Col. Bogey's March." Soon others join in, until all are whistling in unison — their morale soaring to new heights in the teeth of catastrophe. The smoking stops. The Guards dog-trot their precious cargo to the door where the First Guard turns back to make a flamboyantly obscene gesture. They go. Casement, sullenly quiet until now, springs to his feet in a fury of indignation.)

CASEMENT. Your Lordship! May I speak?

SMITH. You may *not! (Canny.)* Unless you are sworn. After that, you may say anything you please.

READING. Do you wish to be sworn?

SULLIVAN. He does *not!*

CASEMENT. May I challenge on a point of law?

READING. Let's hear it.

SMITH. Milord, he is not in the court to instruct us in the law!

CASEMENT. The Crown Prosecutor knows exactly why I'm here! Better than anyone! I'm here because your government is morally bankrupt. I'm here because the Irish Home Rule Bill — already on the statute books — was blotted out again. I'm here because I took the only course left for an Irishman after that treachery!

SMITH. That is *not* a point of law, Milord. If he wants a pulpit, let him build a chapel!

READING. This court has been very patient, Sir Roger, but —

CASEMENT. Not as patient as Ireland, Milord! Twenty seven ago you pledged to grant her independence. And *still* that pledge — made in your name — is not fulfilled!

SMITH. But what is the point of law?

CASEMENT. I tried to sit silent, Milord, while the mightiest legal minds of the kingdom haggled, like fishwives, over a misplaced comma. I came to this high court to have my life choked out of me with a rope — not to be parsed to death by pedants!

SMITH. Are you quite finished, Sir Roger?

CASEMENT. It's too early to say.

SMITH. Milord, these interruptions are intolerable!

READING. This court decides what will and will not be tolerated. I see that emotions are running high. And the hour is late. I will rule on the Treason Statute when we reconvene. This High Court of

Justice stands in recess until ten o'clock tomorrow. *(Others wait, respectfully, for Reading to leave the bench before dispersing. Lights cross-fade to Blackwell's office. His Page [also the Chorus] enters with unwelcome news.)*
CHORUS. She won't leave without seeing you, Sir Ernley.
BLACKWELL. *(Wearily.)* Oh, very well ... show her in. *(The Chorus brings Gertrude in and goes.)*
GERTRUDE. Sir Ernley, the Crown Prosecutor says my request for a visitor's pass was referred to you.
BLACKWELL. My dear Miss Bannister. We've allowed you into the courtroom where you can see for yourself that the defendant is being treated fairly.
GERTRUDE. I wish to speak to him privately ... on family matters. What is the status of my visitor's pass?
BLACKWELL. I sent it on to the Home Secretary with my recommendation.
GERTRUDE. What did you recommend?
BLACKWELL. My communications with Mr. Samuels are "privileged." He is always free, of course, to ignore my advice.
GERTRUDE. Has he ever done so?
BLACKWELL. Come to think of it ... I don't believe he has.
GERTRUDE. Please, Sir Ernley, Roger has been like an older brother all my life ... making me do my lessons ... always encouraging me to be independent and persistent —
BLACKWELL. He succeeded admirably.
GERTRUDE. I owe Roger everything. Now in his hour of greatest need ... he must think I have abandoned him.
BLACKWELL. As well you might, under the circumstances.
GERTRUDE. *(Alert.)* What circumstances?
BLACKWELL. You do know, of course, that your beloved Roger is a practicing ...
GERTRUDE. What?
BLACKWELL. *(Backs off.)* Revolutionary.
GERTRUDE. That's not what you started to say. A practicing *what?*
BLACKWELL. Since you force the issue, Miss Bannister, I deeply regret having to show you these. You recognize the handwriting? *(Gertrude glances at the paper.)*
GERTRUDE. Yes. What are they?
BLACKWELL. Pages from his "personal" diary. *(She reads. He*

watches for her reaction. There is none. She hands them back.) Perhaps now you understand, Miss Bannister, why we have kept you — and all decent, respectable people — away from him?

GERTRUDE. *(Grim.)* Do you think I am an idiot child to be taken in by this obvious slander? Or to accept your pathetic pretext for keeping us apart?

BLACKWELL. I understand your loyalty. In a way, I respect it. But it is badly misplaced. You, yourself, vouched for his handwriting.

GERTRUDE. Roger could not possibly be what these pages suggest. He has scores of lifelong friends — men and women. And not *one* has ever doubted his moral character for an instant.

BLACKWELL. Yes, his friends *are* remarkably tenacious. But we are still investigating.

GERTRUDE. To say nothing of Roger's *enemies!* All of those envious Oxford colleagues in the Foreign Office. There isn't *one* who didn't resent being passed over while an upstart *Irishman* rose to knighthood. They would have crucified him!

BLACKWELL. You don't understand Foreign Office protocol, Miss —

GERTRUDE. And what of the speculators? The investors who lost out when Roger exposed their abuse of native labor on the rubber plantations? So many enemies — all eager to find anything to discredit him — and *not one* ever suspected? Ever breathed a word of this scandalous behavior going on day after day? *(Scolding school teacher.)* Really, Sir Ernley! Is this the *best* His Majesty's government could contrive to blacken Roger's name? Frankly, I am embarrassed for you. I will expect a pass waiting for me when I visit Roger tomorrow. Good day! *(Gertrude turns and walks out. Blackwell is left muttering to himself.)*

BLACKWELL. What a remarkable woman … *(Lights fade in the office and come up in the courtroom, in session.)*

READING. With regard to the Treason Statute of 1351, over five centuries of precedent cannot be ignored. The indictment stands. If there are no further motions, we will now hear closing argument for the Crown. *(Smith goes to the exhibit table and unfurls a large green flag with Limerick Castle centered on it.)*

SMITH. Gentlemen of the jury, despite repeated attempts by the prisoner and his able counsel to divert you with irrelevant matters, the case for the Crown is a simple one. This prisoner, blinded by a hatred of England as malignant in quality as it was sudden in origin, has played a desperate hazard. Played it — and lost. Today the forfeit is claimed. Let us review what has been proved. This is the flag he brought ashore when he crawled up out of the salty flotsam of Tralee Bay. Does anyone recognize this flag? Of course not.

JONES. The Empire of Germany recognizes it.

SMITH. *(Irked.)* What do you hope to gain by that interruption, Mr. Jones?

JONES. Accuracy.

SMITH. *(Sarcastic.)* Is that all?

JONES. Isn't it enough? *(Jones acknowledges guffaws around the court with a shy grin and sits. Smith's frown hardens.)*

SMITH. Yes. Germany recognizes it. That gives us a fair notion of its worth. *(Smith flings it on the floor. Sullivan is on his feet.)*

SULLIVAN. Your Lordship!

READING. Mr. Sullivan?

SULLIVAN. I am Irish, myself!

READING. Yes, Mr. Sullivan?

SULLIVAN. *(Swallowing hard.)* Nothing, Your Lordship.

READING. Continue, Mr. Smith.

SMITH. Gentlemen, you have here a knight of the realm who accepted royal honors with the obsequious flattery of a courtier. A knight who pledged his humble duty to his Sovereign. A government official who retired — on *pension.* What has happened since to corrupt him, I cannot say. One thing is obvious, however, the Sovereign to whom he pledged that duty ruled over a great and wealthy empire — unequalled in resources, mighty in majesty, at peace with the world, seemingly unassailable. But today, that same nation is struggling to retain her possessions, her honor, her very existence in the most prodigious war ever to test human fortitude. And *this* is the very hour Sir Roger chose to strike his Sovereign a treacherous blow from the back — a rebellion in Ireland.

CASEMENT. *Incredible!* After methodically slaughtering Irishmen for over seven centuries, the Crown Prosecutor expects us to apologize for reacting in haste! *(Smith fires an accusing finger.)*

SMITH. You swore personal obedience to the Crown when you accepted knighthood!

CASEMENT. That's true. I nearly became an Englishman. During the Boer War, I was well on the way to being a Jingo for the Empire. But, finally, in the forests of the Congo, where I found the true face of King Leopold, I found myself, as well. I had been looking at the tragedy of Ireland through the eyes of the English race. But later, far up the Sulanga River, after watching the brutal butchery of helpless natives there, I knew I could not return home and turn a blind eye to the endless butchering of Ireland.

SMITH. Milord! This is my summation! Kindly silence that rebel!

CASEMENT. If I'm a rebel, you made me one! We Irish have suffered a more prolonged series of evils — deliberately inflicted — than any other community of the civilized world. When men must beg for leave to subsist in their own land, to sing their own songs, to garner the fruits of their own labor, then surely it is the saner, braver course to be a rebel. Wherever it leads. Even here. *(Directly to Smith.)* To think, Freddy, that you were once an Irishman. *I* am not the traitor here. With all the titles and honors the Crown will heap on you, I would not exchange my lofty place in this prisoner's dock for yours groveling at the foot of the throne.

SMITH. Change places with *you?* Hardly.

READING. Sir Roger! This is neither the time nor the place to vent your personal animus toward the Crown Prosecutor. *His* actions did not bring you here. He raised no "Irish Brigade."

CASEMENT. Your government, Milord, told us to lay down our arms at home and take up yours in a foreign war. Why? So that your great and wealthy Empire might grow greater and wealthier. But even if your war had the high moral aims claimed for it, it would *still* be our sacred duty to disobey. If we must fight a war to save the small nations — as you claim — we will fight under the green banner that I see trampled in this courtroom, for our *own* nation — at *home! (Smith is worried by the Juror's respectful silence, as Casement sits again. He tries another tactic.)*

SMITH. How passionately the prisoner speaks on behalf of the impoverished Irish people. How he suffers for them. What hypocrisy! Speaking as he does with the King's lifelong pension in his pocket.

SULLIVAN. To clarify that point, Your Lordship, Sir Roger earned every shilling of his modest pension by faithful service — often at great personal risk — in the jungles of the Congo and the Amazon. Regrettably, the malarial swamps there broke his health and forced his retirement. The pension referred to was a mere four hundred and twenty-one pounds which he renounced more than two years ago. It sits today in the King's treasury — unclaimed.

SMITH. *(Nettled.)* I did not interrupt to clarify *your* remarks.

SULLIVAN. Perhaps there was less opportunity. *(An appreciative chuckle in the court, forces Smith to a more devious tactic.)*
SMITH. What has *perverted* that man's character from its early promise, I dare not guess. What it was that *seduced* his private energies, causing them to *degenerate* from lofty principle to *vulgar practices,* I may not speak. It is like a grotesquely *inverted fairy* tale, the way this prisoner's affections have *descended* to the *basest* —
SULLIVAN. *(Up and furious.)* Your lordship! I most vigorously protest that kind of thing!
READING. *(Innocently.)* What kind of thing, Mr. Sullivan?
SULLIVAN. The way he is characterizing the defendant.
READING. This is closing argument. He is entitled to characterize the defendant.
SULLIVAN. It's not what he's *saying.* It's what he's *implying!* He is deliberately planting innuendo in the juror's minds with those suggestive words, Your Lordship.
READING. Which words do you mean, Mr. Sullivan?
SULLIVAN. Well … I don't wish to repeat them. Those words with ambiguous meanings.
READING. Read back the Crown Prosecutor's last remarks.
SHORTHAND CLERK. *(Flat monotone.)* " … What it was that seduced his private energies causing them to degenerate from lofty principle to vulgar practice I may not speak."
READING. Is that the passage you meant?
SULLIVAN. It was largely in the *way* he said it — his *emphasis.*
READING. Sir Frederick, did you intend ambiguous meanings?
SMITH. No, Milord. I have always tried to speak only the best *Queen's* English.
SULLIVAN. The expression is *King's* English!
SMITH. I've heard it both ways. Is the matter of *gender* on trial here, Milord?
SULLIVAN. There! You see? He did it *again!*
READING. Jurors are instructed to give a literal interpretation to the Crown Prosecutor's remarks. You are not to find any hidden nuances in his words. Does that content you, Mr. Sullivan?
SULLIVAN. With all due respect, Your Lordship, it does *not.* A vile assertion, prejudicial to my client, has been cleverly introduced into these proceedings by the Crown's advocate.
READING. Then specify your objection, so that I may rule.
SULLIVAN. The learned Prosecutor knows full well I cannot *spec-*

ify his poisonous innuendoes without further prejudice to my client.
READING. Do you wish a conference in chambers?
SULLIVAN. No, Your Lordship. The mischief was done *here* — and *here* it must be set right.
READING. Mr. Sullivan, I have allowed you considerable latitude in the conduct of your defence, but this vague request —
SULLIVAN. Very well! Very well! With the court's indulgence, I will endeavor to specify. Even my learned adversary will concede that there are certain words which, though innocent in one context, may be quite damaging in another.
SMITH. Such as?
SULLIVAN. We need no more examples after the display you just put on! *(Approaches Reading, imploring.)* Your Lordship, the prisoner's private behavior — *alleged* behavior — can have no bearing on this trial. It happened — is *alleged* to have happened — years ago … when Sir Roger was in … in the … uh … Consular Service … *(Sullivan's attention is distracted by Blackwell, who stands, opens the black diary found in Casement's trunk, and flips through it.)*
BLACKWELL. "April sixth … April seventh … April eighth … "
SMITH. *(Sudden outrage.)* Mr. *Sullivan!* Do you realize what you're doing?
SULLIVAN. What…?
SMITH. You are pleading your case *within the bar!* Since his Lordship is too courteous to reprimand you, let me remind you that it is a serious breach of court etiquette for a *junior* barrister, like yourself, to move at any time within the bar. *(Sullivan, a stickler for decorum, is aghast at his infraction and nearly leaps out of his skin getting outside the bar.)*
SULLIVAN. *(Badly rattled.)* I had forgotten momentarily … I beg the court to understand that in my anxiety for my client … That is, to understand that no disrespect was intended.
READING. The court is not offended, Mr. Sullivan. Proceed.
SULLIVAN. I'm exceedingly grateful, Your Lordship. It shall *not* happen again. You — you — you may be confident of that.
READING. Please continue, Mr. Sullivan.
SULLIVAN. Yes … quite … I was saying that Sir Roger was still in the Consular Service when certain behavior — *alleged* behavior … *(When Blackwell moves directly behind Sullivan to read in his ear, Sullivan walks away and covers his ears. But Blackwell follows. The scene shifts back to the jury room with them.)*

BLACKWELL JUROR. "April ninth: Very hot today. Indian boys swimming naked all afternoon. Lovely bodies flashing in the stream."
SULLIVAN JUROR. Mr. Foreman! Make him stop doing that!
BLACKWELL JUROR. "April tenth: Aridomi followed me like a dog all afternoon. Gave my breeches to him. Has beautiful, smooth, coffee-colored limbs."
READING JUROR. You're looking a bit green around the gills, old chap. Better sit down.
SULLIVAN JUROR. Not until I make my point. The issue here is *treason!* Not whether Sir Roger is or isn't …
BLACKWELL JUROR. "April eleventh: Rain all morning. Ears ringing from quinine. Went to meet mail boat. Lovely olive-skinned sailor. Seventeen. Very shy at first."
SULLIVAN JUROR. Please stop reading that *filth!*
ROBINSON JUROR. He's right. You look pasty. Not your fault. Some people just aren't cut out for jury duty. It takes balls.
BLACKWELL JUROR. "April twelfth: More rain. Will miss sailor's incredible warmth. Native boys willing, but do not quiver with eagerness. Dear Taki and two sweet friends all night consoling me. One very stiff and large."
SULLIVAN JUROR. All right! All right! I'll change my vote! He's *guilty!* The man is *guilty! (Sullivan Juror slumps over a table, completely broken down. Blackwell Juror smiles and puts aside the diary.)*
ROBINSON JUROR. *(Scornful.)* That still leaves us with *one* "not guilty." *(All eyes turn toward Casement Juror, who stands apart from the others.)*
SMITH. Maybe not. I propose another ballot.
M.P. JUROR. Wot's the use? 'E'd rather 'ang this *jury* than one bleedin' poof!
HALL JUROR. We might take a voice vote and drown him out.
ROBINSON JUROR. I'm for that!
M.P. JUROR. That's the ticket, Gov!
SMITH JUROR. Does anyone object to a voice vote? *(Some hostile Jurors surround Casement Juror, daring him to object.)*
BLACKWELL JUROR. I object.
M.P. JUROR. *You?*
ROBINSON JUROR. But you was *for* conviction all along!
BLACKWELL JUROR. I still am. But he has a right to dissent. *(With a groan, the Jurors throw up their hands in disgust and walk*

away.)

CASEMENT JUROR. I'd like to thank you.

BLACKWELL JUROR. Don't. I'm your worst enemy.

CASEMENT JUROR. At least I know where you stand.

BLACKWELL JUROR. Do you?

CASEMENT JUROR. I *tried* to vote for conviction on the last ballot.

BLACKWELL JUROR. Did you now?

CASEMENT JUROR. I actually wrote down "guilty." But when I tried to fold the ballot and pass it up … it wouldn't fold. The paper turned into an iron plate right in my hands.

BLACKWELL JUROR. Interesting.

CASEMENT JUROR. And when I changed my vote to "*not* guilty" … it folded easily. I can't imagine why.

BLACKWELL JUROR. Can't you? Have you never wondered why you developed this curious, compulsive attachment to Sir Roger? Others will. *(Blackwell Juror turns with an enigmatic smile and walks away. Casement Juror hesitates a moment, then follows, grabs Blackwell Juror, and spins him around.)*

CASEMENT JUROR. *(Indignant.)* It's not true!

BLACKWELL JUROR. Perhaps not. But "appearance" is everything, isn't it?

CASEMENT JUROR. I vote "not guilty" because I believe it. No other reason. And I won't have my good name sullied by anyone here! *(Other Jurors are attracted by this outburst.)*

M.P. JUROR. What *was* your name again, Gov?

CASEMENT JUROR. West. Ernest West.

ROBINSON JUROR. Oh, yes. From Willesden, wasn't it?

CASEMENT JUROR. That's right. What of it? *(M.P. Juror grabs his wrists and turns up his palms.)*

M.P. JUROR. It's obvious you don't *work* with these! What do you do in Willesden, then? *(Casement Juror jerks free and stands his ground against his cynical tormentors.)*

CASEMENT JUROR. I am a head schoolmaster.

ROBINSON JUROR. Wot kind of school is it, then?

CASEMENT JUROR. I don't know what you mean. A school is a school.

M.P. JUROR. I don't agree at all. To tyke an example, it might be a *military* school.

CASEMENT JUROR. It's not.

M.P. JUROR. No. Come to dwell on it, you ain't exactly the *military* type. *(To Robinson Juror.)* Would you say?
ROBINSON JUROR. Military? No. Definitely not military.
M.P. JUROR. Let's see now … that still leaves quite a collection. Is it a *trade* school?
ROBINSON JUROR. Or a *maritime* school?
M.P. JUROR. Or an *orphanage* school?
ROBINSON JUROR. Or a *mechanical* school?
M. P. JUROR. Or a *painting* school?
ROBINSON JUROR. Or a *dancing* school?
M.P. JUROR. Or a *codfish* school?
CASEMENT JUROR. It's a *private boys' school!*
M.P. and ROBINSON JURORS. *(Simultaneous.)* Nooooooo?
M.P. JUROR. 'Ear that? 'E's headmaster of some private boys.
ROBINSON JUROR. No, no, no! 'E's headmaster of some boy's privates.
M.P. JUROR. That's not wot 'e said, at all. Mind yer tongue!
ROBINSON JUROR. It's not *my* tongue we're talkin' about!
M.P. JUROR. You didn't 'ear 'im right. Wot 'e said was 'e's master of the schoolboy's private 'ead.
ROBINSON JUROR. Same thing!
M.P. JUROR. Not the same. You got a filthy mind, ya' know that? *(Casement Juror begins to retreat under their bullying, but they keep after him.)*
ROBINSON JUROR. I know wot I 'ear! Go on, Gov. Tell 'im 'oo's right. Tell 'im wot you are once more.
M.P. JUROR. And try to speak up loud an' clear, this time.
CASEMENT JUROR. *(Unsettled.)* It's a highly accredited school. One of the best in London. A boys' preparatory school.
ROBINSON JUROR. There! You see? It's a boys' preparatory school.
M.P. JUROR. Aye. But wot is 'e preparin' the boys' *for?*
CASEMENT JUROR. A *useful* life! A *productive* life!
ROBINSON JUROR. 'E means a life where a bright lad can *shoot* ahead … by fallin' behind every now and again … if ya' know wot I mean.
CASEMENT JUROR. This is *monstrous!* Beastly behavior!
M.P. JUROR. Look who's callin' us "beastly."
ROBINSON JUROR. I do believe we struck a nerve. *(In groping about for support, Casement Juror appeals to Blackwell Juror.)*
CASEMENT JUROR. You! You're a sensible man. Tell them we

can't condemn a fellow human being to death with mockery like this. It's *undignified!*

BLACKWELL JUROR. He's absolutely right. A human being deserves better.

CASEMENT JUROR. There! You hear?

BLACKWELL JUROR. However, I'm not certain that would include Sir Roger.

CASEMENT JUROR. *(Stung.)* Not even … human?

BLACKWELL JUROR. Not in any civilized sense. His diary proves that he has been addicted for years to the most loathsome and bestial sodomitical practices. *(Now that the bully-boys have softened him up, Blackwell Juror moves in for the kill.)*

CASEMENT JUROR. The diary may not even … be his…?

BLACKWELL JUROR. The handwriting matches up.

ROBINSON JUROR. 'Ere's a page from 'is putrid diary. See for yourself! *(Casement Juror shoves the paper away.)*

CASEMENT. That wouldn't prove anything. It could be forged.

BLACKWELL JUROR. By whom? And why?

CASEMENT JUROR. I don't know … *(Grasping straws.)* Sir Frederick, perhaps. They're bitter enemies from way back. Or Naval Intelligence. They have forgers on staff, don't they?

BLACKWELL JUROR. Do they?

CASEMENT JUROR. I've heard that. People who make up fake German passports and documents for our spies to use. Those people.

BLACKWELL JUROR. All that trouble to discredit one, troublesome Irishman?

CASEMENT JUROR. They tried to hang Parnell with forged letters when the Home Rulers got too strong. Why not Casement? *(Blackwell Juror is stopped cold for a moment, as this sinks in.)*

BLACKWELL JUROR. No forger was convicted in the Parnell case.

CASEMENT JUROR. Because he ran off to Spain!

BLACKWELL JUROR. And Parnell took off with another man's wife!

ROBINSON JUROR. Well, Sir Roger won't chase anyone's *wife.* That's clear enough. Here, see for yourself. It won't bite you.

CASEMENT JUROR. I won't look at that!

ROBINSON JUROR. " … Olive-skinned sailor. Seventeen. Very shy at first. Lovely, long one. Ten inches at least."

CASEMENT JUROR. *(Covers ears.)* I won't *listen* to it, either!

(Blackwell Juror waves the others away, then gently pulls Casement Juror's hands away to reason with him.)
BLACKWELL JUROR. He *wants* to die an Irish martyr. Don't you see?
SMITH JUROR. The only way he can redeem his blunders now is at the end of a rope. He's depending on us to put him there.
HALL JUROR. That's why we must bring in a "guilty" verdict.
CASEMENT JUROR. I don't believe that. Nobody *wants* to die.
(Smith, Hall and Blackwell Jurors exchange a conspiratorial look. Clearly a different tactic is needed.)
BLACKWELL JUROR. I'm not sure you quite grasp the point. There is no prospect that he'll actually *hang* because of our verdict.
CASEMENT JUROR. But they killed Pearse and the other rebel leaders...?
SMITH JUROR. In the heat of emotion, yes.
HALL JUROR. And *neither* was a knight of the realm.
BLACKWELL JUROR. He has too many friends in high places to be hanged.
SMITH JUROR. Not after a widely publicized trial.
HALL JUROR. The fact that he's "dying" to become an Irish martyr, is more than enough to keep him alive.
CASEMENT JUROR. I hadn't considered that...?
BLACKWELL JUROR. They're bound to reprieve him with all the clemency petitions.
CASEMENT JUROR. You really think so?
BLACKWELL JUROR. Of course. Think of the pressure from America, alone. And just when Whitehall is courting them to join the war.
SMITH JUROR. With all the Irish in the States, would England *dare* to hang one of their favorite bloody heroes?
HALL JUROR. At worst, they might tuck him safely away in prison 'til after the war.
BLACKWELL JUROR. And even that's not certain.
SMITH JUROR. Our verdict is a mere technicality.
HALL JUROR. It has to be filed, so the appeals may get underway.
CASEMENT JUROR. In that sense ... I'm actually standing in his way.
BLACKWELL. Precisely how I'd view it.
SMITH JUROR. And I.

HALL JUROR. And I. *(Casement Juror looks around at the three nodding heads. He writes on his ballot, offers it to Smith Juror, then has sudden misgivings and won't let go. They both tug on it.)*
SMITH JUROR. Let's have it, then!
CASEMENT JUROR. No! *(Casement Juror snatches back the ballot and walks quickly away toward the cell area. Morton Juror follows after him.)*
SMITH JUROR. Do we have a verdict or not? *(When Smith Juror starts after Casement Juror, Blackwell Juror stops him.)*
BLACKWELL JUROR. He may wriggle a bit. But the hook is in deep enough.
SMITH JUROR. Do you suppose he *is* a pervert?
BLACKWELL JUROR. West, here? I haven't the foggiest. He *is* a moral coward, of course. But that's hardly a distinction these days.* *(Lights cross-fade from the jury room to the prison cell, where Casement looks from Morton to the paper in his hand.)*
CASEMENT. Seeing this obscenity … in my own handwriting … I know what true depravity is. This upsets me, Dick.
MORTON. I'm sorry, Roddie. I thought you'd want to see what they're showing around.
CASEMENT. I should have guessed from the aspersions — none too subtle. From my sentry here. People on the street as I passed by in irons. Even in the courtroom.
MORTON. Now that you know, what are you going to do about it?
CASEMENT. Nothing.
MORTON. *Nothing…?*
CASEMENT. *(Burst of anger.)* There's nothing I *can* do! Don't you see that? It's done.
MORTON. That's bloody nonsense, Roddie! You can *deny* it! You *must* deny it!
CASEMENT. How long have we known each other? Twenty-five — thirty years? Half our lives! And you tell me I have to deny *this!*
MORTON. For your own good! Yes!
CASEMENT. No!
MORTON. Why not?
CASEMENT. Because it should never have come up!
MORTON. Of course not! But it *did.* And simply ignoring it won't make it go away.

* Optional text may be inserted here. See Appendix.

CASEMENT. Neither would *denying* it!
MORTON. Perhaps not ... but saying nothing leaves the rest of us ... your friends ... helpless to defend you.
CASEMENT. Yes, I see that, dear old friend. I didn't stop to think how awkward it must be for you. You should stay well out of it.
MORTON. How can I? After you crawled up on Banna Strand and claimed you were *me!*
CASEMENT. Did they question you?
MORTON. Did you think they *wouldn't?* They came to the house. In the middle of the night. May was upset for days after.
CASEMENT. I'm sorry, Dick. I wish there were something I could do.
MORTON. There *is!* Deny this filth they forged into your diary! If not for your own sake, then for your friends!
CASEMENT. Friends don't need a denial, Dick. The rest won't believe one. I've spent forty years fighting lost causes. I'm not going to end my life in the ultimate futility of trying to dissuade my enemies from what they are so eager to believe.
MORTON. I'm not suggesting you debate it in Commons — just make a simple statement in the courtroom.
CASEMENT. No.
MORTON. Why, Roddie? Why? *(Casement glances again at the paper and shakes his head, resigned.)*
CASEMENT. I'll say it once more. Then I'd rather not discuss it again. Whatever my private life may be — and you know it as well as anyone — it has no bearing on this trial.
MORTON. You know, of course, that your silence will make those filthy lies more relevant.
CASEMENT. *Believed,* perhaps. Never *relevant! (Casement calmly tears the paper in half — twice — then drops it on the cell floor.)* Now, my oldest, dearest friend ... truce? *(Casement holds out both arms. Morton embraces him, stiffly, then turns and leaves without another word. As Casement stares dejectedly after Morton, the Chorus enters behind him, humming to himself. He starts to sweep up the torn paper with a push broom, sees Casement's frown, shrugs apologetically, and sweeps silently out of the cell. Lights dim on the cell, as the Chorus sweeps down to the apron and leans on his broom.)*
CHORUS. Let's see ... have we left out anything? The trial's over. Convicted, of course. Nothing now but to wait out his last days in the condemned cell at Brixton until — *(Looks at an audience member.)*

Sorry? … His *sentence?* … Oh, I thought you knew. *(The Chorus turns upstage, points to the high bench area and snaps his fingers. Lights pop on. But no one is there.)* Well? *(He raps the broomstick impatiently on the floor several times. A flustered Reading rushes on from the wings, robe flying and peruke askew. He pauses at the bench to regain his dignity, then abruptly pantomimes hanging himself with both hands around his own neck, one elbow straight up, eyes crossed, tongue dangling out.)* Thank you! *(The Chorus raps the broom once again. Lights go out at the bench. Reading makes a dignified exit.)* This is where all the clemency appeals pour in. One from the Archbishop of Canterbury, no less. And petitions for pardon from around the world. Even a sternly worded "Sense of the Senate" resolution from Washington. But *nothing* is going to save Roger from the rope — not while those high government muckety-mucks have a few more dirty cards left to play. And they *do.* You'll see. *(He starts to broom his trash offstage, but pauses as he passes Casement in the dark cell.)* For his part, I think Ruari Macasmunde is ready. All he wants now is to make his peace with God and the few friends he has left. Here comes one now. *(The Chorus leaves. Lights come up in the cell where Gertrude hesitates, then goes in. Gertrude faces him, uncertain, for several moments before Casement holds out his arms and she rushes into them.)*

GERTRUDE. I tried everything. I was afraid they'd never let me see you.

CASEMENT. Your leave of absence hasn't been very restful. The girls at St. Anne's will be glad to have you back. *(Sees her frown.)* What? What is it, Gee?

GERTRUDE. *(Covering up.)* Nothing.

CASEMENT. Remember the pledge we made as children never to lie to one another? Tell me, Gee.

GERTRUDE. I got a cable yesterday. I've been dismissed from St. Anne's.

CASEMENT. *Damn* them! They had no right!

GERTRUDE. Actually, I was getting a bit tired of the pampered darlings at St. Anne's. I'll find another position where —

CASEMENT. You *loved* St. Anne's. How could you *not* after so many years?

GERTRUDE. I'll manage. What matters is that *you* persevere. You must show these petty-minded government toadies what a true Irishman can endure.

CASEMENT. *(Wryly amused.)* You haven't changed in the least.

We might still be children at play ... invincible ... heroic ...
GERTRUDE. That's what you *are* to me, Roger. To the Irish everywhere! A hero! You can't change that. You mustn't. We need you now ... more than ever.
CASEMENT. I'm no hero, Gee. I've made awful mistakes — done heaps of things wrong.
GERTRUDE. But think of what you did *right!* In the Congo. In Brazil. In raising the Irish flag so high at the trial it was seen all around the world! Your childhood dream of glory, Roger ... it's come true!
CASEMENT. There can be no lies between us, Gee. You agreed to that ... *insisted* on it.
GERTRUDE. I know, but —
CASEMENT. There's a truth you have to know about me. If I don't tell you now ... *(She holds his stern gaze as long as she dares, then looks away.)*
GERTRUDE. Nothing you say could change my opinion of you.
CASEMENT. The truth is, Gee, that your devoted cousin, the hero of your childhood fantasies is actually ... *(Pauses, reflects long and hard.)* Such a *coward* that he tried to poison himself.
GERTRUDE. Oh, no, Roger!
CASEMENT. With a packet of curare sewn into my jacket. I rubbed it into a cut finger and got violently ill. I lay delirious in my own vomit all day. There's your great Irish hero, Gee. *(Gertrude frowns until her fertile imagination comes to the rescue.)*
GERTRUDE. You did it to protect others — so the British couldn't torture their names out of you.
CASEMENT. My, dear, sweet, *devoted* cousin. You can't think *anything* ill of me. What will you do when I'm — when this is over with?
GERTRUDE. Please, Roger. I can't think of that now.
CASEMENT. I want you to promise something.
GERTRUDE. Anything ... you know that.
CASEMENT. Don't leave me in this dreadful, dreary place. Take me home. Let me lie in the old Murlough churchyard overlooking the bay.
GERTRUDE. I'll see to it ... I promise ... *(She is near tears, as lights cross-fade from the cell to Smith's office. Sir Edward Grey is waiting there, impatiently winding his pocket watch. Smith's Secretary [the Chorus] looks apologetic.)*
CHORUS. I can't think what's keeping him, Sir Edward. I put your appointment on his calendar myself.

GREY. Five minutes. Then I have business at Whitehall.

CHORUS. Of course, Sir Edward. *(The Chorus nods, deferentially, as he backs toward the apron, then turns to the audience, pointing over his shoulder.)* Sir Edward Grey ... Foreign Secretary ... and a genuine friend of Sir Roger. He's not a bit happy. Not to mince words — he's *pissed* with Sir Frederick! You'll see. Here comes "Galloper" now. Shhhh ... *(The Chorus tiptoes off, quiet as a mouse, as Smith hurries in and parks his cane.)*

SMITH. Terribly sorry, Eddie. I forgot you were coming.

GREY. Is it true?

SMITH. Probably. What isn't these days? Would you share a discreet brandy with me?

GREY. You blocked Roger's final appeal to the House of Lords?

SMITH. I did ... yes. The jury was out for barely one hour. I call that a clear-cut verdict.

GREY. To convict, yes. But surely there are grounds for clemency?

SMITH. None that I'm aware of.

GREY. To convict was a matter of course. But to *hang* him can only cost us the good opinion of neutral countries that could be vital to our war effort.

SMITH. You think womanly sentiment will impress them? I doubt it. Neutrals will join the side with the stiffest backbone.

GREY. Mercy is not a weakness.

SMITH. No. But a *luxury* in time of war.

GREY. An appeal to the House of Lords is *expected* when an exceptional point of law is involved.

SMITH. There *isn't* one in this case.

GREY. There *is* according to the leading historian of British law. Professor William Holdsworth was most vehement on the point. I assume you're familiar with his reputation?

SMITH. *(Faint smile.)* Quite familiar. Willie was runner up to me when I won the Vinerian Law Scholarship at Oxford. *(Grey is stopped cold by this. He stalls for time to regroup.)*

GREY. I believe I *will* take that brandy, after all.

SMITH. Excellent! It's older than both of us. And mellower. *(Grey sips slowly, then tries a different approach.)*

GREY. You know, Freddy, cynics may conclude that you blocked Rogers's appeal for "personal" reasons. Why bear such undeserved reproach, when the Lords stand ready to ratify your judgment?

SMITH. It *is* distressing, Eddie, to be so grossly misjudged. But

knowing that I have the good opinion of informed friends, like yourself, makes it bearable. *(Grey holds his gaze, sips, then asks.)*
GREY. Was it absolutely necessary to use his diary to pollute his memory?
SMITH. Absolutely. We are at war, Eddie. Total, all-out war.
GREY. There are civilized rules — even in war.
SMITH. Yes. *All* made by the victors. *(Grey puts down his glass to leave.)* You mean you aren't going to ask?
GREY. Ask what?
SMITH. If his diary was forged.
GREY. *(Cutting.)* It doesn't matter. What you have *done* with it is a far greater obscenity than anything that could possibly be written in it. *(As Grey walks off in disgust, Smith calls curiously after him.)*
SMITH. You never give up, do you, Eddie? Where to now?
GREY. If the Lords can't hear an appeal, there is always the royal pardon! Have you thought of *that!*
SMITH. *(To himself.)* Yes … as a matter of fact, we have … *(Lights brighten in Blackwell's office as he finishes penning a memorandum. He looks it over, nods, hits the call-bell on his desk and seals the document. A young Page [the Chorus again] materializes at once.)*
CHORUS. Sir?
BLACKWELL. Take this straight to the Home Office and hand it to Mr. Samuels personally. You understand?
CHORUS. Yes, Sir.
BLACKWELL. This is a highly sensitive matter. No one else is to know what I have recommended to the Home Secretary. Is that clear? *(The Chorus gives the audience a conspiratorial glance before answering.)*
CHORUS. Oh, yes, Sir. Perfectly clear, Sir.
BLACKWELL. Carry on, then. *(Lights fade on Blackwell's office and follow the Chorus down to the apron, as he unseals the document.)*
CHORUS. This should be worth a peek, don't you think? The Home Secretary is the only one left standing between Sir Roger and the hangman. He could arrange a royal pardon for Sir Roger, but *only* if it is recommended — in writing — by his chief legal advisor — Sir Ernley Blackwell. *(Clears his throat and reads aloud.)* "Casement's diary proves that he has come full circle — from a pervert to an invert — a *woman* or *pathetic* who derives his satisfaction by inducing young men to use him. I believe the diary is a faithful and accurate record of his behavior, just as it occurred. It would be

wise to allow the law to take its course and — by judicious means — circulate his diary to prevent Casement from attaining martyrdom." *(The Chorus shrugs at the audience, appalled at the depths of human depravity. He reseals the document, as he walks away. Lights come up in the condemned cell. The Prison Governor is preparing Casement for execution. A Warder [the Chorus] enters and assists.)*

CASEMENT. What a beautiful day.

GOVERNOR. Yes. St. Stephen's Day.

CASEMENT. *(Wryly amused.)* The martyr. At least the *end* of my life will be fitting.

CHORUS. Open your shirt collar, Sir. *(Apologetic.)* For the rope.

CASEMENT. Of course. *(The Prison Doctor, a gaunt man with a black satchel, enters and faces Casement.)*

DOCTOR. Is there anything I can do for you?

CASEMENT. Nothing, Doctor. Thank you.

DOCTOR. Something for your nerves, perhaps?

CASEMENT. I've never felt more composed. *(The Doctor leaves, passing Father Ryan, who hurries in waving a paper.)*

RYAN. From Cardinal Bourne. The Church embraces you.

CASEMENT. Good. May I see it? *(Ryan pushes a pen into his hands.)*

RYAN. Your signature is needed to confirm it … just there. *(Casement starts to sign, hesitates, then frowns at the paper, as he reads:)*

CASEMENT. " … Hereby expresses deep repentance for his impious public behavior and his *odious private acts* — " I can't sign this!

RYAN. You are a heterodox Catholic, Roger. You *must* sign it — or perish without the Mother Church.

CASEMENT. But "odious private acts"?

RYAN. We have *all* done things we are ashamed of.

CASEMENT. But my enemies will use this against me!

RYAN. Love your enemies, Roger. "Do good to them that spitefully use you and persecute you."

CASEMENT. I'm giving them my *life!* Isn't that *enough?*

RYAN. It will be their ultimate triumph, if you let them drive you from the comfort of the Church. Sign it as an act of submission — a test of your own faith. God knows the truth. *(Casement's face hardens. He hands back the paper.)*

CASEMENT. I will die with my sins. Let them *live* with theirs.

GOVERNOR. Sir Roger, you have time for a final visitor, if you wish. A Mr. Morton is here.

CASEMENT. Good old Dick. By all means. *(The Governor*

motions Morton forward, then draws the others aside.)
MORTON. Roddie ...
CASEMENT. I love you like a brother, but if you cry now I will never speak to you again.
MORTON. I'll behave.
CASEMENT. Do you bring news?
MORTON. Yes. From your bank manager.
CASEMENT. Overdrawn again?
MORTON. No, your drafts are covered. But he can't *read* them. He insists that you stop writing them in Gaelic.
CASEMENT. Gaelic is the only language musical enough to make the paying of debts tolerable. If he weren't a typical, stiff-necked, bloody-minded Englishman, he'd know that.
MORTON. *(Mock scolding.)* You forget, Roddie ... *I'm* English.
CASEMENT. No, you're a poet. Poets are aliens — *wherever* they live. *(They run out of emotion-hiding banter, leaving Morton emotional again.)*
MORTON. Is there anything I can do for you, Roddie?
CASEMENT. Remember the day I received word of my knighthood? With you and May at your place in Denham?
MORTON. Yes. You spoiled the whole week-end fretting over it. You nearly turned it down. May and I had to beat it through your thick skull that you could end the beastly treatment of Peruvian natives faster with a "Sir" on your name.
CASEMENT. Don't forget that, Dick. Someday my ghost may call on you and demand that recollection. I'll come clanking up the avenue —
MORTON. Clanking?
CASEMENT. I'll be in armor. Look at the date — 1351. I'll ask — in Norman-French — if one Dick de Morton lives there. Then I'll demand your memory — or your head!
MORTON. Try not to frighten May.
CASEMENT. Dear May ... give her my love. I treasure you both.
MORTON. I know ... Roddie ... *(The Warder [Chorus] leads Morton away. The Governor looks at Casement.)*
CASEMENT. Yes. I'm ready. *(Lights dim on the small procession, as it leaves the cell and winds its way slowly toward the high gallows level. A bright spotlight picks out a dotty, old man balanced precariously on top of a ladder with a huge book on his lap. We are in the Records Office with the Keeper of the Rolls. A young Clerk [the Chorus again]*

steadies the ladder.)

KEEPER OF ROLLS. Eh, Lad! Which Honor's List does His Majesty say there? *(The Chorus unfolds a formal-looking document with many seals attached.)*

CHORUS. Companion to the Order of Saints Michael and George.

KEEPER OF ROLLS. Hm … Michael and George … Michael and George … *Yes!* Here it is. "Roger David Casement." Bold as life. Now, where the bloody hell did I put — ? You got a rubber down there, Lad?

CHORUS. Right here, Sir! *(The Chorus hands him an eraser. The Keeper of Rolls attacks the open book with such vigor it rocks the ladder.)*

KEEPER OF ROLLS. It's a lot of nonsense, if you ask me. Put in a name. Rub out a name. They ought to make up their frigging minds — and let the rolls be. *There! (The Keeper of Rolls blows the eraser crumbs right into the Chorus' face.)*

CHORUS. Hey! Careful up there!

KEEPER OF ROLLS. Clean as a whistle! You'd never guess to look at this Honor's List that Sir Roger was — *(Adjusts his bifocals.)* Oh, shit!

CHORUS. Anything wrong, Sir?

KEEPER OF ROLLS. I've degraded the wrong knight.

CHORUS. Noooo?

KEEPER OF ROLLS. Oh, yes I have, too. Took out the name right above his, I did. *(Clucks his teeth.)*

CHORUS. Well, put it back in — quick! That's the official record!

KEEPER OF ROLLS. I don't know who it was. He's gone now. All trace of him. Let's just keep this little lapse to ourselves, shall we? A tight lip and a bright eye. That's how to get ahead, Lad. And someday *you* might be Keeper of the Rolls, eh? *(The Keeper of Rolls cackles and attacks the book again, shaking the ladder. Meanwhile, the dimly-lit procession arrives at the gallows, where a masked Executioner awaits them. Lights dim there as Executioner ties Casement's wrists.)* What was that other date, then, Lad?

CHORUS. He was made a knight bachelor on June 20, 1911. *(The Keeper of Rolls covers his eyes with one hand and flips to the back of the book. He looks at the page and beams.)*

KEEPER OF ROLLS. Heh, heh. How do you like *that,* eh, Lad? The *exact* page!

CHORUS. Luck!

KEEPER OF ROLLS. Luck my arse! Training, my boy! Years of

training! Righto! There's the very bugger I want, too!

CHORUS. You ought not to call him *that,* Sir!

KEEPER OF ROLLS. Lord forgive us. What a prissy crop we're growing now. There's the *rotter,* then. "Roger David Casement, C.M.G." We'll soon take care of *that.* Where's that rubber, Lad?

CHORUS. Up your arse …

KEEPER OF ROLLS. What's that? What did you say?

CHORUS. I said, behind your ear!

KEEPER OF ROLLS. Oh — so it is! I'll get him on the first go this time! *(With a gleeful, geriatric cackle, he launches into a frenzy of spastic erasing that nearly topples the ladder. Lights up on the scaffold. Executioner finishes lashing Casement's feet.)*

CASEMENT. Strange. Now that I stand face to face with it, I feel as if you are about to kill a child. My hands so free of blood … my heart so full of compassion for others … I cannot imagine why anyone should wish me dead.

RYAN. *Wait!* I will accept Sir Roger into the faith without the Cardinal's faculty.

CASEMENT. No, Father. I won't have you punished on my account.

RYAN. Every priest has discretion at the point of death. *(Father Ryan takes out a small cruet of holy water and impresses a baptismal crucifix on Casement's forehead.)*

RYAN. By the jurisdiction accorded to all priests, *in articulo mortis,* I receive Roger David Casement, a child of God and a member of the faithful congregation, back into the Church Temporal, that he may enjoy the intercession of all saints and aspire to life everlasting. Amen.

GOVERNOR and WARDER. Amen.

RYAN. *In nomine Patris et Filii et Spiritus Sancti.* Amen. *(The Governor, nods. The Executioner tries to put a hood over Casement's head.)*

CASEMENT. Must you?

GOVERNOR. In case you weep.

CASEMENT. I am not ashamed to weep for Ireland. *(Executioner waits for the Governor to nod then puts away the hood. He pantomimes adjusting a noose around Casement's neck. Smith walks into an isolated pool of light downstage and is joined by Blackwell.)*

BLACKWELL. Well done, Freddy. Or should I say … "your *lordship?*"

SMITH. *(Surprised, pleased.)* Not so, Ernley?

BLACKWELL. England may have faults. But ingratitude is not

among them. His Majesty spoke of a "First Lord of Birkenhead," I believe.

SMITH. Soon?

BLACKWELL. When present emotions have run their course.

SMITH. Quite. And the diary?

BLACKWELL. Impounded for fifty years. Then fifty more, if necessary.

SMITH. Couldn't they be destroyed?

BLACKWELL. That would look as if we had something to hide. Let the system manage it until people forget. They always do. That's really what keeps the system going, isn't it? Ta-ta. *(Blackwell exits, pleased with himself. Smith rolls the words around on his tongue, enjoying the sound of it.)*

SMITH. "First ... Lord ... of Birkenhead." Yes ... Yes, indeed. *(Beginning softly, the Chorus strums "Rule, Britannia," as Smith makes lordly strides offstage. A tight pin spot comes up on Casement's upper body. The Executioner makes a final adjustment of the noose and steps back. On the line: "Britains never, never, never will be — " the last word is cut off by the loud clatter of a sprung trap. Casement's head jerks to one side. His body twists slowly on an invisible rope. As the pin-spot irises down to Casement's shoulders, then his face, and finally out, the Chorus strolls down to the apron singing the last bitter stanza of the opening ballad.)*

CHORUS.

Aye, they stripped you of your honors
and they hounded you to death
And their bloodlust was not sated
as you gasped your dying breath.
They tried to foul your memory
as they burned your corpse with lime.
But God is not an Englishman
and truth will tell in time.

So, like I said before, I have *my* views of this matter. And you, no doubt, have *yours.* Either way, it's comforting to know that all this was long ago. And that high-muckety-mucks today — yours and mine — would never think of engaging in such skullduggery as that. *(The Chorus smiles and starts away strumming. He stops and looks back, concerned.)* We *are* all comforted by that thought, aren't we? *(He breaks into an impish grin, salutes the audience and exits, strumming his guitar.)*

End of Play

APPENDIX

The following text is optional for performance. It can be inserted on page 73, where the asterisk appears.

BLACKWELL JUROR. West, here? I haven't the foggiest. He *is* a moral coward, of course. But that's hardly a distinction these days. *(Smith, Hall and Blackwell sit at a small side-table near a large potted fern and begin playing cards. NOTE: We are in transition to the future this time. The men are relaxing in Blackwell's exclusive London club playing with absurdly oversized cards — every one of which is an ace of spades. Other Club Members drift about like shadows in the background with drinks and cigars. A pantomimed billiard game draws several kibitzers nearby. The sound of clicking billiard balls is heard from time to time.)*

HALL. Ernley, is there any real likelihood of a pardon, do you think?

BLACKWELL. Good Lord, no. Not the slightest.

HALL. What about the clemency petitions? There are half a dozen going around, you know?

BLACKWELL. Nine have reached the Home Secretary, so far. Ten, if you count Bernard Shaw's solo effort. *(Considers a card play.)* I'm not sure any does … *(Makes the play.)* … except Bernard Shaw, of course.

SMITH. They have some impressive names.

BLACKWELL. Indeed, yes. The Archbishop of Canterbury, for one. Though his ardor cooled a little when Casement asked for a Catholic prison chaplain to discuss his *next* conversion.

HALL. Isn't he Protestant?

BLACKWELL. Now and then … but there seems to be a Catholic baptism in the early records, as well. It appears he laid off his bet with the Almighty.

HALL. Poor fellow never has found his niche.

BLACKWELL. He's made some remarkably tenacious friends, all the same. The quality of signatures on his behalf is extraordinary — considering the diary has circulated two months already.

HALL. On *both* sides of the Atlantic.

BLACKWELL. It indicates that people have grown less contemptuous of — *(Blackwell interrupts himself as a Club Waiter arrives with unwrapped cigars on a silver salver. Blackwell draws one slowly under his nose, and smiles.)* Cuban … Oriente Province … excellent bouquet. Do try one, gentlemen. *(Hall and Smith take cigars which the Club Waiter lights for them.)* Thank you, John. These will do fine. *(Club Waiter leaves.)*

HALL. You were saying…?

BLACKWELL. Was I?

HALL. What the petitions indicate…?

BLACKWELL. Yes. That people have grown *less* contemptuous of sodomites or *more* contemptuous of us. I'm not at all certain which.

SMITH. I really have to admire your style, Ernley. Even here — between the three of us — you speak as if his diary were completely authentic.

BLACKWELL. *(Deadpan.)* You speak as if it *weren't. (Smith glances between the two impassive faces studying their cards.)*

SMITH. We were sitting in my office at the time.

BLACKWELL. At what time?

SMITH. When we all agreed to it. *(Blackwell considers a play narrowly, then makes it.)*

BLACKWELL. Do you know what he's talking about, Reggie?

HALL. No idea.

BLACKWELL. Nor I. Your play. *(Hall plays a card.)*

HALL. I remember the meeting at your Commons office, Freddy. We discussed the Treason Statute.

BLACKWELL. And which prison to put him in. Anything else, Reggie?

HALL. No. That was it.

BLACKWELL. *(To Smith.)* Your play, then. *(Smith nods with understanding, then plays a card. Blackwell takes the trick.)* Yes, indeed, we are witnessing a remarkable change in social attitudes, gentlemen. Imagine it — poets and prelates signing the *same* petition…?

HALL. That business about Whitehall not daring to offend President Wilson I thought particularly effective.

BLACKWELL. Thank you.

HALL. I don't suppose there *is* any risk from that quarter?

BLACKWELL. None whatever. President Wilson is from *Northern* Irish stock. Ulster, I believe. Besides, he's seen the diary.

SMITH. That leaves only the threat of a Senate resolution.

BLACKWELL. Come now, Freddy. The Senate? A threat? It's hard to imagine that benign debating society a serious threat — resolved

or unresolved. *(Considers card play.)* Hm … a trick to you, Reggie.
HALL. *(Plays.)* Amazing. How did you know? Not a marked card, by any chance?
BLACKWELL. *(Pretending injured feelings.)* Reggie … I'm crushed. You *know* I never cheat anyone who can be beaten fairly. It's a matter of strict principle with me. *(Lights cross-fade from the jury room to the prison cell, where Casement looks from Morton to the paper in his hand.)*

PROPERTY LIST

Guitar
Water pitchers, glasses
Briefs, satchels
Blank ballots
Writing utensils (notepads, pens, pencils, eraser)
Train ticket stub
Rubber surgical gloves
Torn notepaper
Newspaper
Old black ledger
2 pocket watches
Sealed letter
Rifle
Statute books
2 walking canes, 1 of which doubles as a flask
Snifter
Cigar
Manuscript
Folded diary pages
Treaty
Bayonet
2 letters
Large brown envelope containing photocopies
Wastebasket
Large yellow-tinted glass document case
Thermometer
Clipboard
Jeweler's loupe
Heavy law book
Large green flag with Limerick Castle on it
Push broom
Memorandum
Call-bell
Document with several seals attached
Rollbook
Bifocal
Rope
Cruet of holy water

SOUND EFFECTS

Crash of surf
Loud banging of trunks being broken into
Loud rapping on a door
Rain and thunder
Thunderclap
3 signal bell rings

www.ingramcontent.com/pod-product-compliance
Lightning Source LLC
LaVergne TN
LVHW020250181026
850497LV00043B/933